PLANNING
YOUR MODEL RAILROAD

Tony Koester

KALMBACH BOOKS

WAUKESHA, WI

Acknowledgments

It takes a sizable support group to produce a book on a multifaceted topic. I extend my sincere appreciation to those who provided information and photos, including Jeff Aley, Joe Atkinson, Don Ball, Jim Bennett, Bruce Black, Erik Block, Chuck Bohi, Mike Bowline, Jim Boyd, Broadway Limited, Mike Brock, Jack Burgess, Chesapeake & Ohio Historical Society, Joe Collias, Mike Confalone, Chuck Conway, Evan Daes, Bill Darnaby, Rick De Candido, Gene Deimling, Mike DelVecchio, Richard Deuso, Paul Dolkos, Darrell Finney, Kip Grant, Steven Grigg, Dan Holbrook, Gary Hoover, Gene Huddleston, Tom Johnson, Randy Laframboise, Andy Keeney, Jim Leighty, Steve King, Bill Kloss, Jeff Kraker, Dale Kreutzer, Daryl Kruse, Tom Maule, Allen McClelland, Marty McGuirk, James McNab, Lance Mindheim, Lee Nicholas, Jim Odell, Dave Olesen, Ted Pamperin, Jim Providenza, Mike Schafer, Jim Six, Bob Sobol, Bob Springs, Perry Squier, David Stewart, Brooks Stover, J.W. Swanburg, Rich Taylor, Jay Williams (Big Four Trains), and Craig Wilson. Special thanks are once again extended to Jeff Wilson and his Kalmbach Books' boss, Dianne Wheeler, who guided this book through Kalmbach's meticulous production process.
Tony Koester

On the cover

Linden, Ind., is a key junction town on Tony Koester's Nickel Plate Road layout. Planning key towns, structures, and elements is an important factor when planning a layout.

About the author

Planning Your Model Railroad is Tony Koester's 13th book about scale model railroading. Tony has been the editor of *Model Railroad Planning*, a special annual issue of *Model Railroader* magazine, since its inception in 1995. He is a contributing editor to MR, writes the popular Trains of Thought column, and has written numerous feature articles. His current multi-deck HO railroad, which accurately depicts the Nickel Plate Road's St. Louis Division as it appeared in 1954, is fully operational and scenicked. Tony resides in Newton, N.J.

Kalmbach Books
21027 Crossroads Circle
Waukesha, Wisconsin 53186
www.KalmbachHobbyStore.com

Published in 2015
19 18 17 16 15   1 2 3 4 5

Manufactured in China

ISBN: 978-1-62700-229-5
EISBN: 978-1-62700-176-2

Editor: Jeff Wilson
Book Design: Tom Ford

Library of Congress Control Number: 2015930766

Contents

A plethora of options

It's difficult indeed to plan something without a clear vision of where we're going. When it comes to planning our next model railroads, for example, there are almost limitless choices. So Job One is obviously going to be narrowing those options down to a select few, preferably only one. In Chapter 1, we'll therefore examine three broad-brushed opportunities covering the range of options from anything-goes freelancing to strict adherence to modeling a specific prototype in a tightly defined place and time. In subsequent chapters, we'll discuss how to get there from here, looking at choices you'll make regarding benchwork, models, level of detail, size and style of layout, and many other factors.

Harder is easier

Strange as it may seem, the more effort you expend to narrowly define your objectives, the easier they are to achieve. For example, I am modeling the (take a deep breath) Third Subdivision of the St. Louis Division of the Clover Leaf District of the New York, Chicago & St. Louis Railroad, better known as the Nickel Plate Road. More specifically, I

am modeling nine towns located along about eight scale miles (roughly 500 feet in HO) of that subdivision in the fall of 1954, the last full year of steam operation and, more specifically, the last fall grain rush using steam power. That's pretty specific, but a few of my friends are modeling a specific month of a specific year. At least one has narrowed it down to a specific day!

That may seem impossible to implement, but it is actually quite liberating. In my case, by modeling autumn 1954, I know what equipment I can or cannot run. If a car on my railroad is stenciled with a NEW date prior to, say, November 1954, it's probably good to go. Alas, all of those beautifully detailed Kadee PS-2 covered hoppers are out of reach, as they carry 1955 and later built dates; I'll have to focus my limited hobby budget elsewhere.

I occasionally hear that such strict adherence to a narrowly defined time line is inhibiting rather than liberating. A more broadly defined timeline offers far more choices when acquiring equipment and even structures. The downside is that one may therefore

succumb to whim buying and wind up with what we call a Home Hobby Shop—shelves of kits and ready-to-use models that will never turn a wheel on our railroads. If you enjoy collecting models, that's good; if you find yourself short of funds for more important stuff, that's bad.

There are other key decisions facing the layout planner: single or multi-deck benchwork being a major one. The photo at right clearly shows my choice for a point-to-point, multi-deck railroad. Except at one discrete spot (which varies with the viewer's height) as the railroad gradually climbs westbound, neither deck is at an ideal height. Offsetting that is that I achieved two complete "laps" around the basement, thus doubling my mainline run and greatly enhancing the layout's operational capabilities.

Dropping back a step, you may be asking yourself about the virtues of continuous-run vs. point-to-point, or even an island layout (think 4 x 8 sheet of plywood) vs. around-the wall.

Addressing the myriad sides of such concerns is the raison d'être for this book, so let's get started!

So many choices: scale, gauge, era, single- or multi-deck, focused on realistic operation or primary a scenic tour de force, one-horse short line or mainline racetrack. My steam-era HO railroad exemplifies a walkaround design on a multi-deck layout (see the December 2014 *Model Railroader*). This view shows the 24"-wide lower-deck "bump-out" to accommodate the L-shaped Nickel Plate Road-Monon depot at Linden, Ind. On the 16"-wide upper deck, two trains are meeting at the east end of Metcalf, Ill. The panel is a same-size replica of the one on the NKP operator's desk that controlled the interlocking plant. The depot is now a museum.

1

CHAPTER ONE

This way, that way, or down the middle?

Clearly in flagrant violation of the old adage not to have the main line run parallel to the edge of the benchwork, the main line through Metcalf, Ill., on my HO railroad is dead straight for a scale three-quarters of a mile. This affords a dramatic look at oncoming westbound trains as, with Mars lights flashing a stern warning to motorists, they hustle freight and passengers from central Indiana toward St. Louis in the autumn of 1954—and the autumn of steam on the St. Louis Division.

Defining and then refining your objectives is the first task we'll tackle. But I need to ask a favor: Keep an open mind. If you come to this discussion with a pre-determined set of objectives, you'll almost certainly miss opportunities that lie outside of your chosen path. An example of the flexibility you may need is a mismatch between your operating objectives and the railroad—more specifically, the segment of a railroad—you want to model. Example: The increasing popularity of timetable and train-order operation strongly embraces a long, single-track main line, **1**.

6

2 Tom Maule used U.S. Geological Survey topographic maps to accurately model the narrow-gauge Mann's Creek both horizontally and vertically. His railroad is located upstairs in a full-size "model" of the MC's car shop. *Tom Maule*

Degrees of freelancing

To some extent, we're all freelancers. I can think of only one modeler who has modeled an entire railroad inch for inch; even his elevations are accurately depicted, **2**. Almost all of the rest of us have bitten off more than we can possibly chew.

I'm modeling a 111-mile-long subdivision. That's roughly 586,000 feet. Divide by 87.1 for HO scale miles, and it would require a mainline run of a mere 6,700 feet—this in my roughly 30 x 60-foot basement. That's not gonna happen, even with a wedding-cake cascade of decks starting on the floor and extending up to the ceiling.

With the design talents of Frank Hodina and three decks, we did manage to achieve an 8-scale-mile run between the two division points of Frankfort, Ind. and Charleston, Ill. I am therefore modeling about 7 percent of the Third Sub, but pretending I'm modeling the entire subdivision.

As the crew of westbound second-class freight No. 45, the KC Local, prepares to leave the passing track at Linden, Ind., to continue their run over the Third Subdivision on the author's railroad, they cannot see around the corner. They must therefore consult the schedule published in the employee timetable to see whether they can safely progress to at least the next passing track against superior (by direction) eastbound trains.

There's no mistaking the capabilities and hence the appeal of modern diesel-electric locomotives. Daryl Kruse models the Union Pacific's ex-C&NW main from Chicago across the Mississippi River on this long bridge to Clinton, Iowa, in N scale. *Daryl Kruse*

Allen McClelland weathered this pair of Alco RS-11s to show that they work hard for their keep on his HO Virginian & Ohio. They look the part despite a lack of superdetails such as individual grab irons or a flashy paint scheme. Everything on the V&O was detailed to a consistent level. *Paul Dolkos*

Is that enough? Fortunately, the percentages don't count for much. My main goal was to have enough towns but not too many towns. That is, since the Third Sub was a single-track, timetable and train-order (TT&TO—more on that in Chapter 3) railroad, we needed a half-dozen or more places where inferior trains could duck out of the way of superior trains—eastbound trains being superior on most railroads.

But we also needed for the towns, hence passing tracks, to be sufficiently far apart so that crews could not simply cheat and look ahead to see whether the way is clear, **3**. Rather, they had to check the timetable schedule against their superiority, or lack thereof, and any train orders that helped or restricted their movements. In a nutshell, that's the whole point of TT&TO operations, which was a primary reason I modeled that particular stretch of the Nickel Plate.

You, on the other hand, may be enamored with the battleship-sized wares of General Electric and Electro-Motive seen on today's railroads, **4**. Those beasts are extremely impressive to watch and to hear in action. But they also tend to pull equally impressively long trains.

Noted British layout designer Paul

Lunn said that he continues to be amazed when clients tell him that they have already chosen a modeling scale before they have located a place for their railroad-to-be. Do you have enough space for a railroad capable of supporting your favorite type of motive power and train length? Are you willing to change from, say, HO to N or even Z scale to enable such trains to be modeled?

Refining the term "freelancing"

Even those modelers called "rivet counters" are still freelancing to some degree owing to practical constraints. The distinction between prototype modeling and plausible freelancing is more about one's attitude and goals than it is about physical limitations of space, time, budget, and so on.

In fact, you may be at a relatively early stage of your interest in scale model railroading and simply don't know enough about "prototype" (full-size—but not "real," please, as models are equally real!) railroading to see a marked difference.

I suspect that most modelers lean toward the freelancing side of the spectrum. They may not know enough about prototype railroading to be able to refine their modeling to the point where a knowledgeable observer could tell at a glance what, when, and where their railroads are situated. They may

6

My Allegheny Midland was designed to connect the Nickel Plate Road in southeastern Ohio with Allen McClelland's Virginian & Ohio in Virginia. Here the Low Gap Shifter heads up the branch across the Coal Fork bridge with mine supplies and empty hoppers.

want the freedom to express themselves artistically or simply do not care about accuracy to that extent.

There is no point system that rewards prototype fidelity. But I'll argue that it either is or is likely to become important for the neophyte to do his or her due diligence as over time, perhaps even by default, he or she learns more about full-size railroading.

Think of it this way: To communicate, we need a common language. I'm writing this book in American English,

but that doesn't mean you will understand the essence of what I'm trying to convey. We both need to speak North American Model Railroading as well as North American Railroading—both technical, highly specific languages—to truly understand one another.

More to the point, unless you understand what I'm trying to convey and why I think it's important for you to consider it, we have both failed—me as a teacher and you as a student.

7

A Key brass Berkshire from the 1980s and a Walthers Proto 2000 plastic Berkshire of recent vintage show how well detailed today's ready-to-run locomotives can be. Can you tell which is which? (NKP no. 707 is the brass model.)

During and immediately following college, Bill Darnaby amassed a fleet of Monon first- and second-generation diesels such as this boiler-equipped Century 420—only to realize their presence meant the end of the type of operation he preferred. Bill then created a freelanced railroad with the desired characteristics. *Bill Darnaby*

After the Monon dieselized in the late 1940s, it immediately started to run longer, hence fewer, freight trains. This saved money but, for the model railroader, the lighter traffic density makes it less challenging to operate the railroad under timetable and train-order rules. Here 132-car No. 72 behind five F3s is leaving Bloomington for Lafayette, Ind., in June 1963. *Kenneth Ardinger*

Matching goals to layout size

Brooks Stover models the shortline Buffalo Creek & Gauley and its connection with the Baltimore & Ohio in West Virginia in S scale (1:64). Of necessity, he kitbashes or scratchbuilds a lot of his motive power, including massive Baltimore & Ohio 2-8-8-0 EL-3 no. 7136 (top), which he kitbashed from a Lionel 2-8-8-2 with a scratchbuilt tender. He also scratchbuilt the body for B&O Alco RS-1 no. 9185 (above right) from styrene. His track plan and the overview photo (right; also see *Great Model Railroads* 2011 and the December 2009 *Model Railroader*) reveal that he limited the size and scope of his railroad to ensure that he had the time to tackle demanding locomotive, car, structure, and scenery building and detailing projects, which Brooks thoroughly enjoys.

10

Modeling a modern regional railroad such as the Iowa Interstate is increasingly popular. It's rewarding to model a railroad you can still see in action. James McNab models the IAIS Grimes Line; the simplicity of the track plan (see *Model Railroad Planning 2014*) allows time for intensive detailing and leisurely operating sessions. *James McNab*

It is therefore impossible for me to provide much help to the true free-lancer. By definition, anything goes in Freelance World, and I have no way of knowing how to address such disparate interests, to find a common ground beyond flanged wheels on two rails. The Davytown & Susieville Railway that runs from an Atlantic port through a series of snow-capped peaks to serve an Unobtainium mine on the Mississippi may entertain its conceiver and builder 'til the cows come home, but I can't offer much specific guidance.

I will therefore assume that you have found that both model and full-size railroading are interesting and worthy of study and emulation. As long as we both agree that a model railroad should be anchored in Reality to a significant degree, we can communicate.

Freelancing is not passé
Do not leap to the conclusion that what I have said in any way denigrates

the idea of freelancing. For a quarter of a century, I had a freelanced railroad in my basement, and I remain proud of what it represented and how it operated. Perhaps half of my closest friends are building and operating model railroads that closely resemble full-size railroads in the region and era they're depicting, but their names and other attributes are not to be found in railroad history books.

Long ago, I coined the term "prototype-based freelancing" to help us understand how such efforts differ from pure freelancing. The term is, I hope, self-explanatory: Such a model railroad exhibits readily identifiable aspects of similar-size railroads in its creator's chosen locale and era. Recently, *Model Railroader* managing editor Hal Miller coined the term "faux-totype." I like that!

One of the most important contributors to defining this approach to scale modeling is Allen McClelland. Back in 1958, he began work on the

first of three HO iterations of his world-famous Virginian & Ohio Railroad. Among those who had tired of fanciful names for model railroad such as the Tweedle & Dee, the V&O leapt off the pages of *Model Railroader* and *Railroad Model Craftsman*, not because it was spectacular but because it wasn't! Rather, "dip-blue" EMD Fs and Geeps and Alco FAs and RS-11s lugged endless strings of look-alike hoppers out of the verdant—but not dramatic or snow-capped— Appalachians, **5**. Modeling Reality had come of age.

I, for one, was so impressed that I designed and built the Allegheny Midland to get on this bandwagon, **6**. Allen and I became close friends, and as editor of RMC (1969–81), I encouraged him to tell us more about the thinking that was behind such a huge step forward for our hobby. That resulted in "The V&O Story" series in RMC, which was later reissued as a soft-cover book of the same name.

11

Joe Atkinson also models the Iowa Interstate and, like James McNab, has limited the size of his railroad so that he can enjoy spending time superdetailing models such as this IAIS maintenance-of-way flatcar. *Joe Atkinson*

Allen's previous experience with model railroading and knowledge of prototype railroading led him to formulate a very clear plan of attack:

He wanted a single-track mountain railroad set in a place that he was very familiar with owing to field trips to the region. He wanted to control it with a Centralized Traffic Control (CTC) system (see 3-7). He knew it had to connect to the rest of the North American rail network and therefore designed the layout with hidden staging yards and interchanges with "foreign" railroads. He wanted train crews to be able to follow along with their trains, which meant building the railroad on shelves along the basement perimeter walls and on a central peninsula. To give crews the required freedom of movement, he had to adapt GE's pioneering Astrac five-channel command-control system to walkaround throttles.

As in any other endeavor, one cannot rest on knowledge, practices, and hardware that were state-of-the-art yesterday. Allen therefore converted to other brands of increasingly sophisticated and flexible command control. Successful as V&O 1.0 was, following a move to a new home, V&O 2.0 exhibited several important enhancements such as a hidden, centralized area where new trains could be made up in real time.

V&O 3.0 is an example of the ultimate in adaptability: building a layout when one has no space whatever for a new railroad. Thanks to his good friend Gerry Albers, who provided space for a sizable segment of the V&O as a major connection for Gerry's Virginian Railway (see *Great Model Railroads 2014*), V&O 3.0 is now fully operational.

This illustrates one of the most important lessons you may derive from this book. As Bill Darnaby, designer and builder of the highly regarded Cleveland, Indianapolis, Chicago & St. Louis—the Maumee Route—once said, "If you really want a model railroad, you will have a model railroad." It may not be the one you dreamed of having, but anything is better than convincing yourself that you can't have a model railroad. Attics, spare or bonus rooms, basements, garages, friends, clubs, modular groups—there is almost always a way!

Prototype modeling

Perhaps you've noticed the trend toward more prototype fidelity in model railroading. It may appear that there is a sea change, that freelancing is no longer in vogue.

It's easy to identify specific reasons for this trend. First and foremost, credit must go to the manufacturers and importers who have listened to knowledgeable modelers. They then produced models that enable the prototype modeler to faithfully depict a given railroad at a given time without spending undue hours detailing each model, **7**. One superdetailed locomotive that represents countless hours of work may fill the needs of a shortline modeler, but it isn't going to do much to improve the roster of a basement-size railroad that could easily require dozens of diesels and/or steam locomotives to keep the railroad fluid. Understanding where your main interests lie and designing a railroad to accommodate them is critical. (See "Matching goals to layout size" on page 11.)

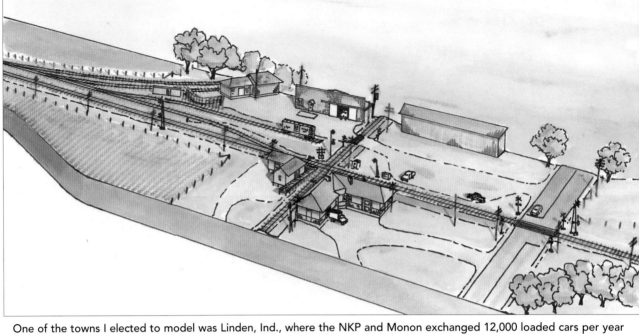

One of the towns I elected to model was Linden, Ind., where the NKP and Monon exchanged 12,000 loaded cars per year and presumably a similar number of empties—up to 60 cars per day! Comparing this initial sketch with a photo of the layout shows that things worked out as planned. The two "wye" tracks behind the gray buildings are each 30 cars long. The NKP delivers to the Monon on the near track, and the Monon delivers to the NKP on the back track. After each 7- to 8-car cut is picked up by the NKP, thus uncovering an infrared sensor and (after a 23-minute delay) activating Iowa Scaled Engineering's Automated Interchange circuit, Monon units on the back track automatically shove more cars into view. The units roll into view after all cars have been picked up.

12

Citing one example, I recall a few decades ago that an early manufacturer (HObbyline) produced a Fairbanks-Morse H10-44 diesel switcher. In the latter part of the last century, Walthers brought out an improved model of that unit, and then improved on that again. Recently, they introduced the same model again, but this time it covers all five versions of the prototype!

This enables the "serious" prototype modeler to have his or her cake and eat it too—an accurate, highly detailed model that out of the box is as good or better than most of us could manage on our own, one that is available for DC or equipped with Digital Command Control (DCC) and sound, and one that can be put right to work without compromising any standards.

When I first met Bill Darnaby at the Purdue (University) Railroad Club, he was modeling the Monon. Some years later, he hosted Monon operating sessions on the progressively designed Midwest Railroad Modelers layout in Batavia, Ill. Then he acquired his own

basement with a house atop to keep out the weather and built a model of ... not the Monon, but the freelanced Maumee Route.

Why the change?

In the time between his building up a sizable first- and second-generation Monon diesel fleet and starting his home layout, Bill discovered the immensely challenging, hence rewarding, timetable and train-order system of operation over a single-track railroad. So all he had to do was to build the Monon's single-track main line, **8**, and operate by TT&TO in, say, the late 1960s, right? Tilt!

The era dilemma

Bill went to work as a mechanical engineer for the Electro-Motive Division of GM, so he understands the impact dieselization had on railroading. The lessons of the steam-to-diesel transition era were by now ancient history, but they were not forgotten: One multi-unit consist of diesel locomotives operated by one train crew

could move a lot more tonnage over the railroad than one crew on a steam locomotive, **9**. As railroads figured this out, they started running longer, hence fewer, trains. The number of interactions between east and west, or north and south, trains thus markedly decreased. That was good for the prototype but very bad for the modeler, as frequent meets are what makes TT&TO so interesting!

The solution was obvious: Move the railroad back into the steam era. That was feasible for those who modeled the likes of the Santa Fe, Union Pacific, or Pennsylvania, but at that time there were no models of Monon steam locomotives—even brass imports—that were available or readily convertible.

Converting and detailing one or two models to match specific prototypes is doable; building an entire fleet of such models is not when you're also tasked with building a basement-size railroad to host them.

So era is an extremely important benchmark: Are the locomotives,

freight and passenger cars, and cabooses needed to depict your favorite railroad in an optimal operational location and time period available and affordable? Are they accurately detailed to a reasonable degree? And do they perform as well as they must—handling long trains up typical grades, for example?

Trade-offs

You can now see how the line between accurately depicting a specific proto-type at a tightly defined time and place isn't simply a matter of declaring your intentions and having at it. Even with the plethora of excellent models from both a railroad-specific appearance and an operating standpoint that are now available, significant obstacles remain.

Modeling some relatively obscure but ever-so-appealing short line or regional, **10**, simply ups the odds against being able to buy exactly what you need. Conversely, since you need fewer of everything, you may be able to afford the time and effort required

to detail generic models to meet your needs, **11**.

The term "stand-off scale" was coined to describe models that look acceptable at normal viewing distance, even though they won't withstand close inspection. This works in the favor of those with large model railroads, as there is so much going on that minute inspections of every car, locomotive, and scene are impractical. It may give you comfort to know that Allen McClelland seldom, if ever, "wasted" time scraping off the molded-on grab irons on his diesel fleet, **5**. Yet despite numerous visits to operate on the V&O, I cannot recall noticing that "omission."

Allen coined the term "good enough" to embrace the larger concept that there is a practical limit to the degree of detail that is required to achieve a certain visual sense of completeness and accuracy. Moreover, everything on a railroad should be brought up to the chosen quality level so that nothing detracts from the

greater whole. If you picked up one of Allen's ancient Athearn F7s, you would see that it looks the part but isn't what you'd call superdetailed. Yet add that same diesel to a three-unit consist lugging a coal train up to Sandy Summit, and it would never occur to you that it lacked anything whatsoever.

Your personal situation

As a group, those of you who fall into the Baby Boomer classification are at an enviable juncture in time. For the most part, you remember when a railroad not only went through your hometown but also had a local freight crew that stopped there to work and to chat with the station agent or tower operator. You remember when every kid asked for a train set for Christmas.

Now that Boomers are retiring in droves, they need a fulfilling hobby. Selling them on the idea that they should consider scale model railroading therefore isn't a hard sell at all. The hard part is finding ways to reach out to them as a group.

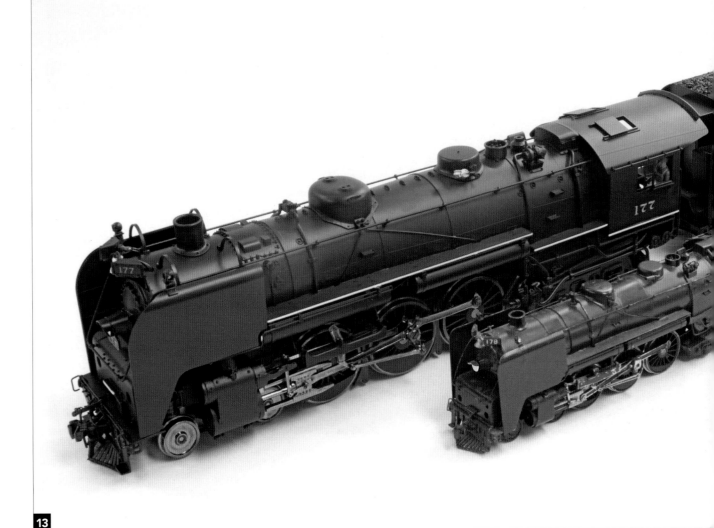

13

The mass of O scale models has an appeal of its own, and the detail of today's products is often both abundant and readily visible. Compare the relative size of a 1970s vintage HO Nickel Plate Products Hudson (right) with a more recent O scale model of the same locomotive from Weaver Models. But working in 1:48 requires either considerable space or scaling down one's aspirations. Modeling a single town fed on one or both ends by a passive staging or active fiddle yard—much like the typical exhibition layout in the United Kingdom and Europe—is one way to model in a larger scale while still restraining the overall footprint to a manageable size.

You may or may not fall into that group. Even if you do, your personal situation will not match that of your contemporaries to any degree. You may face a relocation related to employment or retirement, or one of your children may be moving out (be sure to change the locks!), allowing the repurposing of that space for a layout.

Such changes will have a bearing on the planning of your next, maybe your first, model railroad. It's time to be extremely realistic about what you can and cannot expect to do now and in the future. It's equally important not to allow yourself to be pessimistic

about your prospects. "Where there's a will, there's a way" certainly applies to planning a layout.

Railfan or modeler?

In addition to the distinction between freelancing and prototype modeling, there is another dichotomy that we need to acknowledge: the differing viewpoints of those who are primarily modelers vs. those who are primarily rail enthusiasts.

Like prototype modeling versus freelancing, it's not a black-or-white issue. But decades in the hobby have made it clear to me that there are

modelers whose primary interest is the models themselves, and there are modelers who see the models as a necessary means to an end, not the end itself, as they strive to emulate full-size railroading on a practical scale in their homes or club rooms.

One approach is not necessarily better or more rewarding than the other, but it will have a major impact on one's approach to layout planning. From my point of view as a "coach," it's easier to talk to those who have a keen interest in prototype railroading and spend time at lineside observing the prototype in action. They come to the

table with a lot of hard-won knowledge that the modeler has to learn by rote.

Take sound systems, for example: Most DCC sound-decoder makers advertise their decoders as producing sounds that mimic the EMD 567 or 645, the Alco 539 (with or without turbo), 244, or 251, or one of the General Electric prime movers. The railfan modeler will not only understand this nomenclature but will be quick with an opinion as to the fidelity of each maker's sound decoder. The "pure modeler" (there has to be a better term) may not have a clue or even care as long as it makes machinery noise or chugs and has a bell and whistle or horn.

Those who understand the differences have an edge in that it enhances the realism of their endeavors. And sound systems enhance operations in many ways. For example, I found that the time it takes to move a train out of a yard increases several fold with sound-equipped locomotives as the engineer eases the train into motion to enjoy the realistic sounds. The increased time is equivalent to having a longer railroad.

Plan for ops

The best advice I can offer those who profess no interest in realistic operation is to nevertheless pay close attention to the design attributes that accommodate it. Often, modelers become exposed to operation on someone else's railroad, and most of them begin to understand, hence enjoy, it. You can't expect to embrace something you don't understand, as at the very least it's intimidating and often embarrassing to admit your lack of knowledge.

If you follow the Layout Design Element (LDE) approach to layout design by modeling prototype locations that offer something close to what you envision for a town, yard, and so on, the railroad will not only run plausibly from day one but will be ready and waiting for you to use it realistically as your knowledge base grows, which it almost certainly will.

To clarify: a Layout Design Element, or LDE, **12**, is defined as a visually and operationally recognizable model of an actual place: a town, yard, engine terminal, harbor, large industry, or even a key scene. The idea is to select a few such plausibly related locations as the basis for a track plan. For more details, see my book, *Realistic Layout Building Blocks* (Kalmbach, 2005).

Choosing a scale

Prototype or prototype-based modeling used to be difficult enough without venturing into a minority-interest scale. But today N scale is supported by almost as many model types as HO, and even S and Z scales are growing in terms of equipment being available to meet specific needs.

So the main concern is ensuring that the models needed to populate the railroad you're planning are available in the chosen scale, and that the railroad you envision can be built in the available space.

There's a bit more to it than that, however. How we perceive the size—sheer mass—of models in various scales is highly subjective. HO didn't become the most popular scale solely because of a greater availability of models. Indeed, it was the other way around: Its support by manufacturers and importers is a function of its popularity.

I've built models and model railroads in N, HO, O, and 1:29. But I model in HO. Why is that?

My priorities will differ from yours, but I'm sure we share some common interests and concerns. My aging eyes have long needed glasses to see at distances beyond a few inches, but I can still see unaided all four dots that comprise a full-color printed image. If I had to wear glasses or a magnifier for close-up work, I might decide that O (1/48th actual size) or F (1/20th) scale is more appealing.

Back in 1973, we built a home with a basement that could accommodate a model railroad with a sufficiently long main line in HO scale to meet my operational objectives. Clearly, I could almost double my pleasure if I switched to N. Today, most of the factory-painted models that I would need to depict the same railroad in the same time period are also available in N.

Perhaps I'm just more comfortable with HO. I know from decades of experience that I can detail it satisfactorily. I know it will run reliably. I have an inventory of spare and detail parts. I know what models are available. But I also sense that it has sufficient, well, *mass* to look like a railroad to my eyes. N seems a bit small, but that could be nothing more than prejudice at work.

Going the other way, O scale looks impressively massive, **13**. But I've noticed that many ¼" scale models lack realism because I can see too much—I can tell at a glance that a "wood" model is made of etched brass or molded plastic, as it lacks the needed texture to look like wood.

No matter; I've made my choice. Just be sure you're comfortable with yours.

1

CHAPTER TWO

Basics of
layout design

My HO scale Allegheny Midland provided a quarter century of enjoyment. It was freelanced but tied closely to Nickel Plate Road equipment and Chesapeake & Ohio structures. Both are evident in this view of the coal-marshalling yard at South Fork, W.Va.

Your first concern may be finding a place to put your railroad. I'll agree with that line of thinking, but not in the way you may imagine. When I designed the freelanced Allegheny Midland, **1**, my first step was to find a place for the railroad—on a map! Until I knew where the proposed railroad was to be located, I had no way of planning how it should look, what it should do for a living, what railroads it should resemble, or even what types of locomotives would be needed to deal with the local geography.

When I switched to prototype modeling, I still had to identify not only a prototype but also a tightly defined segment thereof, towns to model, and era, as well as to ensure that needed models were available and could meet performance needs. The Nickel Plate's St. Louis Division out of Frankfort, Ind., met my criteria: It continued to be steam powered through the summer of 1955 and was dispatched by timetable and train orders. *Darrell E. Finney*

When I switched to prototype modeling, **2**, I first had to choose not only a railroad to model but also a manageable portion of it to depict (see "Choosing what to model" at right).

Different but the same

North American railroads have evolved to have a great deal in common. That enables them to interchange freight cars almost seamlessly, making it easy to move a carload of lumber from a sawmill in the Pacific Northwest to a lumberyard in New York (see **3-2**).

Variety is the spice of life, so we're fortunate not to have a national system that clothes everything in a uniform manner. It is the uniqueness of every common carrier that leads us to picking one or a few favorites to study and model.

How we choose a favorite can lead to some missteps. Receiving one of those gorgeous red-and-silver Santa

Choosing what to model

When I decided to build my current model railroad, it was not nearly sufficient to proclaim, "I'm modeling the Nickel Plate Road!" That simple statement led to a host of other questions:

- Which part of the Nickel Plate?
- What division point(s) and town(s) on that segment of the NKP?
- Why those towns?
- What year and season?
- Which scale?
- Are the needed models available or otherwise attainable, affordable, and reliable?
- Does it support the type of operation I enjoy?
- Is enough information available to allow me to model it accurately?
- Will it attract enough modelers

who will regularly attend operating sessions that support the desired intensity and type of operation?

I chose to model the Third Subdivision of the St. Louis Division in the fall of 1954. It was a busy, single-track railroad operated by timetable and train orders; it employed my favorite steam and diesel locomotives, which were commercially available in several scales; I lived along or near this line in the 1950s and '60s and had researched it since I was a child; a good friend who was a knowledgeable and supportive retired professional railroader could serve as my advisor; and there was a historical society (nkphts.org) and several chat groups that focused on the railroad as a whole or this district of it.

Number 9 crosses the Wabash River on its way west from Cleveland to St. Louis on my HO railroad set in the autumn of 1954. Impeccable maintenance allowed the NKP to entrust Nos. 9 and 10 to a single diesel.

Fe F units on a train set for Christmas may make us a lifetime Santa Fe fan. Growing up in a small town may lead us to model the railroad that served that town. Having a relative work for a railroad may make that the home team.

If scale model railroading were nothing more than acquiring and running scale models, that approach would be ideal. Lacking more pressing influences, it usually works out surprisingly well.

But before planting a flag that proclaims ownership of a particular railroad, it pays to reflect on your overall goals and the wherewithal you have to achieve them. Modeling the Pennsylvania, Penn Central, Conrail, or Norfolk Southern multi-track main around Horseshoe Curve in O scale isn't a good idea if you don't have access to a gymnasium.

Lady luck
I got lucky. Really lucky. When I decided it was time to start anew with an HO tribute to a railroad I had studied since my pre-teen years, by pure dumb luck I happened to have grown up along a segment of a railroad that was an almost ideal example of the type of railroading I had become extremely interested in: timetable and train-order operation on a busy single-track main line.

The prototype I chose to model—the Nickel Plate Road—is, like most railroads, an amalgamation of several predecessor railroads. Each of the railroads that merged into the post-1949 Greater Nickel Plate had distinctive characteristics, many of which survived the mergers. Had I chosen a different segment of the NKP to model, I would have had to shift my objectives to match that line's attributes.

Had I wanted to retain the look and feel of an Appalachian coal hauler that was the hallmark of the Allegheny Midland, for example, I would have chosen the southeastern end of the former Wheeling & Lake Erie. The Wheeling tapped into the southern Ohio coalfields.

Been there, done that, however. It was time, I decided, to model a Midwestern racetrack where the NKP's fleet-footed Berkshires (2-8-4s) hustled symbol freights between St. Louis and Buffalo. Bonus: The line hosted two passenger trains, each pulled by an elegant Alco PA-1, **3**.

By talking to former Nickel Plate employees, most notably my good friend and retired NKP engineer Don Daily, I was able to form a very accurate picture of how the Third Subdivision of this line went about its daily toil. It was, as his friend and retired NKP engineer

Bob Curtis told me, a "train-order railroad," which meant that the dispatchers routinely amended the schedules published in the employee timetables to keep the railroad fluid. Superior eastbound freights were routed into passing tracks to avoid making late westbounds even later. Superior but compact passenger trains took the siding to avoid having to stop and, more precariously, start long freights.

In short, it was a perfect railroad to model in the days when steam's reign was nearing an end—assuming one wanted to relearn the archaic art of timetable and train-order railroading, which I most certainly did.

From map to railroad room
I knew where the Nickel Plate's Third Sub resided in time and space. The Allegheny Midland had been dismantled to make way for the NKP in our ample basement. I needed to remove some unneeded stud walls that were fortunately not load-bearing, but otherwise getting started on the new railroad was relatively straightforward.

Not so with the Allegheny Midland. I was and am a great admirer of Allen McClelland and his fabled Virginian & Ohio, and as our friendship grew, I discovered that he was looking for a major connection at the west end of the Afton Division.

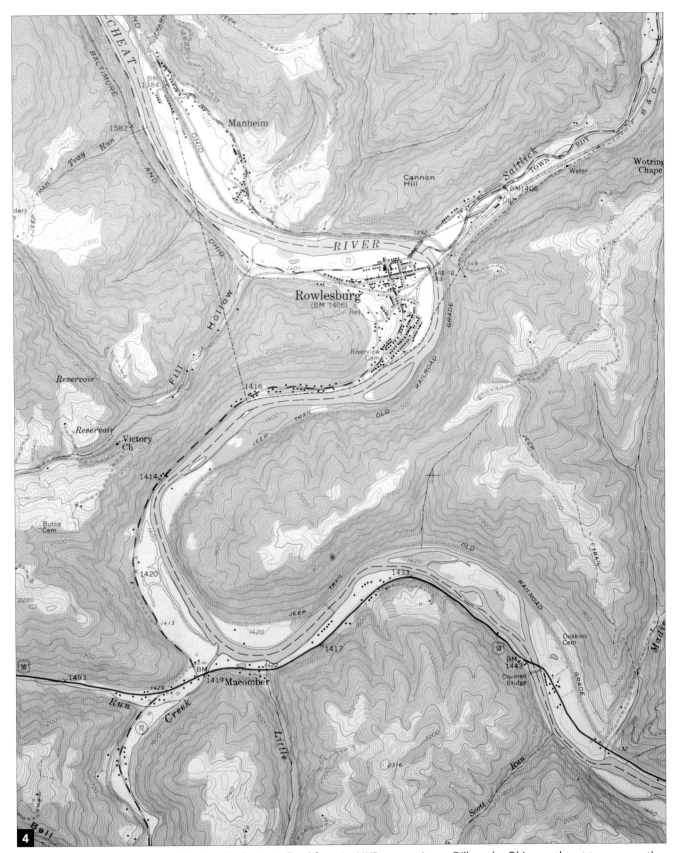

Plotting a plausible right-of-way for the Allegheny Midland from its NKP connection at Dillonvale, Ohio, southeast to a connection with the Virginian & Ohio at Kingswood Junction was a very enjoyable aspect of the railroad's design. After choosing a general route on highway and railroad maps, I refined the routing on U.S.G.S. topographic maps. Here it follows a Baltimore & Ohio line north of Rowlesburg, W.Va., and an "Old Railroad Grade" (Rowlesburg Southern) south of there (orange line) to a connection with the Western Maryland at Parsons, W.Va.

Lighting the lower deck is a primary design consideration on a multi-deck layout. I used under-cabinet fluorescent fixtures with cool-white lamps, but LED strips and fixtures are increasingly popular. The blue "cable" is a rope light for testing moonlit night effects. Feeders run behind the hardboard backdrop to bus wires below the benchwork. Inexpensive stamped metal shelf brackets support the upper deck.

The distance from the point of the frog to the spot where the rails spread one unit apart is the frog number. So if rails spread 1 inch apart 6 inches from the point of the frog, that's a no. 6 turnout. (The switch is only that part of a turnout that moves, so one lines or throws the switch, not the turnout.)

To make this possible, I created a railroad that connected the southeast end of the Nickel Plate (the former Wheeling & Lake Erie, which the NKP leased in 1949) with the west end of the V&O's Afton Division. I rounded up railroad and highway maps of southeastern Ohio, eastern West Virginia, and western Virginia to see whether there might be a semi-plausible route connecting the two railroads. It appeared that by jumping across West Virginia's northern panhandle, heading down the Cheat River, and zigzagging across the ridge that forms the West Virginia-Virginia state line, I could get to Sunrise, Va., just north of a connection with the V&O.

Since I was familiar with geology and land surveying, I went the extra mile and ordered U.S. Geological Survey "quadrangle" topographic maps

7

Jim Six is modeling the Elkhart–Wabash, Ind., segment of the New York Central's branch between Benton Harbor, Mich., and Louisville, Ky. This early version of his track plan shows that it's fed in both directions by a fiddle (active staging) yard that can be switched like a working classification yard. *Jim Six*

for the proposed route. I then plotted the entire route mile for mile where the maps suggested a railroad could have been built. Part of it even followed the abandoned Rowlesburg Southern along the east shore of the Cheat River, **4**.

That the RS was abandoned and the rest of the route barren of railroads suggests my planning may have been more speculative than I then admitted. But—a very important point— the planning was a lot of fun and culminated in field trips to explore the "right-of-way."

I therefore strongly suggest doing due diligence about whatever you are planning if only to determine whether you find that aspect of model railroad design to be a very rewarding process— or sheer drudgery.

Many Baby Boomers who have retired or are about to do so have realized that they need a challenging hobby to keep them creatively entertained for the next several decades. A surprising number of them are building new homes, not to downsize but to provide even more room for the model railroad of their dreams. If not now, when?

But not everyone is fortunate enough to be able to control their destiny to the point where they can build a home around the footprint of a new model railroad. In such cases, it pays to think small. David Barrow has written extensively in *Model Railroader* and *Model Railroad Planning* about his domino concept of sectional layout construction. The idea is somewhat like building a module for a portable railroad like the ones you may have

8

It's easy for the local crew to pick up the tank car at Standard Oil in Cayuga, Ind., via trailing-point turnouts. But picking up the black covered hopper at Jenkins Cement (ahead of the locomotive), reached by a facing-point turnout, will require a runaround move.

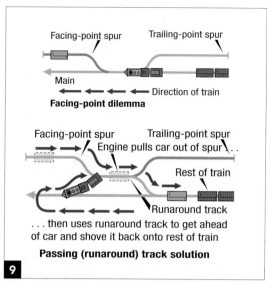

Facing-point spur   **Trailing-point spur**

Main   ← Direction of train

Facing-point dilemma

Facing-point spur   **Trailing-point spur**

Engine pulls car out of spur . . .

Rest of train

Runaround track

. . . then uses runaround track to get ahead
of car and shove it back onto rest of train

Passing (runaround) track solution

9

When picking up a car from a facing-point spur, the runaround track allows the locomotive to pull the car off the spur, leave it on the runaround track, continue to back onto the main line, pull ahead and back up to the car, and then shove it onto its train.

10

This lineup of code 55 (top), 70, 83, and 100 HO flextrack shows the rail height differences. In HO, codes 70 and 83 represent the commonly used 100 and 132-pounds-per-yard rail on full-size railroads. Code 100 remains popular due to its price, ready availability, and ruggedness.

seen at malls around Christmas or at train shows or conventions. But it is different in important ways—the "domino" sections are standardized, but what goes on them is not. If you don't like what you build, tire of it, or have a better idea, scrape it off and start anew!

Combining David's dominoes with the Layout Design Element methodology (Chapter 1) could be an ideal way to get started in planning and building a model railroad, even though you may now have a place to put nothing that's larger than the top of a dresser or bookcase. If the first LDE, perhaps based on your hometown or a site you visited on vacation, works out, then you can build a second, related LDE. And then a third.

Gradually, you will be accumulating the key pieces for a larger home layout; all that's lacking will be the "twisty bits" to connect the LDEs in geographical order if more layout space becomes available. If not, perhaps you can set them up with the help of friends at a model railroad convention or swap meet.

Multi-deck railroads

I wrote a book called *Designing and Building Multi-Deck Model Railroads* (Kalmbach, 2009), so I won't spend a lot of time on that topic here. But it's

an increasingly popular and practical way to get more railroad into the same footprint. Let me offer things to keep in mind as you investigate whether more than one deck will be advantageous: Two decks can be dead level if they are connected by a spiral helix, but a train can spend a lot of "unprofitable" time ascending or descending a helix. If you have enough room for a long main line, the entire railroad (except for towns, which should remain flat) can be a continuous climb, as my NKP is.

Use a bookshelf with removable shelves to test planned layout deck elevations. Have people of various heights view the deck heights and check reach-in distances at several elevations.

Work backward from lower-deck lighting when designing the upper deck, **5** and **9-3**. Don't assume rope lights will provide enough light or a pleasing color; build a test section!

Route all wiring from the upper deck to the bus wires for track power, switch motors, lighting, etc.—which are often best located below the bottom deck—before installing the backdrop. Plan for future needs such as signal detection and lighting.

Install the backdrop on the lower deck after you do the upper-

deck wiring but before you install subroadbed and track.

The good ol' 4 x 8

A classic entry point for new model railroaders tackling their first layout is to buy a 4 x 8-foot sheet of plywood and plunk down an oval of sectional track. As a first step, I'll support that, as anything that gets the trains out of their boxes and onto powered rails constitutes progress.

But I also urge neophytes not to get too comfortable with that arrangement, as they—or a family member—will quickly notice that the "island-type" layout eats up a lot of useful floor space. Worse, unless it is located in the center of a room, thus providing access to all four sides, it will be difficult to reach all sections of the layout for construction and maintenance. Scientific studies have conclusively proven that the farther from the aisle a turnout is located, the more likely it is to cause problems.

A "turnout"? Isn't that called a "switch"? Yes and no. The whole assembly is a turnout, and it is designated by a number that tells how "sharp" it is. A no. 6 turnout has the diverging route crossing the straight-through route at a 1:6 angle. You can determine the frog angle by finding the

11

The end view of two HO trucks (top) shows the narrower code 88 "semi-scale" wheels on the left and the more-common code 110 RP25 wheels at right. Rigid one-piece truck sideframe and bolster moldings with molded plastic spring detail (above) help support narrower code 88 wheels as they ride over flangeways at frogs and crossings.

spot where the rails leaving the frog are spaced one unit apart, then measuring back to the point of the frog; that distance in units is the frog number, **6**. That portion of a turnout that moves is called the switch. So you can't "throw the turnout"; rather you throw or line the switch. And you can't have a "no. 6 switch."

That good ol' 4 x 8 can be repurposed to great advantage. Cut it lengthwise into four 12"-wide, three 16"-wide, two 24"-wide, or one 24"-wide and two 12"-wide strips and arrange them along two or three sides of a room.

Use one section as a staging yard to feed traffic from the North American rail network into the second section, which represents a town, large industry, or yard. Better yet, use two of the three sections to accommodate two staging yards, one on each end of the central town, industry, or yard. That will allow trains to pass through your "one-town railroad," **7**.

The passive staging yards— "passive" meaning rearranged only between, not during, operating sessions—can instead serve as fiddle yards. A fiddle yard, photo **3-5**, is worked in real time—during an operating session—by a separate crew member, often called a "mole" because

fiddle yards may be located in a separate room to reinforce the illusion of trains going to and coming from distant, unseen locations.

Continuous-run or point-to-point?

We've sort of sidestepped a basic question: Should you build a continuous-run or point-to-point layout? I suspect most newcomers to the hobby will prefer a continuous-run design so they can watch their trains go through their paces. That favors a platform plan like the 4 x 8.

But watching the trains go by can become monotonous. Sooner or

O gauge track is gauged at 5 feet rather than the correct 4'-8½". Those who model in O fine-scale, known as Proto:48, correct the gauge error and use wheels that match prototype contours. Compare the locomotive drivers' gauge, width, and flange depth (left). This is especially noticeable on open-frame cars such as hopper cars and tank cars (right), where even the axles are visible. Close attention to track standards is required with P:48. *Gene Deimling*

later, it occurs to most of us that the railroad should be delivering cars to and picking up cars from local industries: a grain elevator, lumberyard, farm-implement unloading platform, retail coal or petroleum dealer, plastics manufacturing plant, brewery, paper mill, warehouse, coal mine, ethanol producer, and so on.

That favors a point-to-point design so that cars are obviously coming from over there and going to somewhere over here. But there's no reason the two staging yards off either end of the main line can't be looped around and connected in one big staging, fiddle, or even classification yard, as Jim Six did, **7**. That will allow continuous run to entertain guests and to test-run motive power, and it makes better use of limited space.

Basic switching needs

At locations where railroads had to do a lot of switching, they often provided a runaround track. It's easy to back into a trailing-point turnout, **8**, to pick up or set out a car. But picking up or setting out a car in a facing-point siding is more difficult. Diagram **9** shows how the car is runaround by the locomotive to position it properly for the required move.

Switching industries in a town or "spots" in a large industry is much easier if the cars are properly blocked (positioned) in the train. At major classification yards, there are usually enough tracks to sort cars in the desired order for the normal destinations: "shorts" for towns in station order for the local freight, and "throughs" for cars going to or beyond the next division point. But only two tracks are needed to do any degree of sorting.

For more information, please refer to my book, *Realistic Model Railroad Operation, Second Edition* (Kalmbach, 2013).

Buying track

What track you choose to purchase may have a direct bearing on the design of your railroad, especially if you do not intend to handlay (build from scratch) turnouts and crossings.

For example, if you choose to use Micro Engineering code 70 track, which has rail that measures .070" high, you're restricted to no. 6 turnouts. If you decide to use code 83 track (.083"-high rail), your options are greatly increased thanks to a wide range of turnouts (straight and curved) and crossings from Atlas, Micro Engineering, Peco, Walthers, and others. Code 100 track is also available in a variety of turnout numbers and crossing angles.

Photo **10** shows the appearance of the most popular rail codes for HO track. Note that the code doesn't change with scale: Code 55 rail is .055" high no matter what the scale or gauge.

Unless you are interested in

13 Large-scale modeling is gradually moving from a solely outdoor activity to one enjoyed indoors as well. I built a 1:29 F-shaped project layout for *Model Railroader* that fit on four standard 30" x 96" folding-leg tables. The bridge (top) is doubled in length by use of a plastic mirror. The mirror also separates the river scene (far-right table in bottom photo) from Claremont, N.H.

The Nickel Plate had both east- and westbound yards at Frankfort, Ind. Switching the westbound yard, as Phil Monat is doing, therefore requires leaning over part of the eastbound side, a task eased somewhat by a raised ledge along the skirting. Roundhouse foreman Rich Taylor (left) and dispatcher Ron Von Werder are discussing engine assignments. In the distance are eastbound yardmaster Jerry Albertie and soybean plant job crew Jeff Ward.

handlaying your track, you need to match your track arrangements to the specifications of commercial turnouts and crossings. The computer-aided design (CAD) programs made specifically for model railroad planning have those geometry options built into their software.

Beginners in HO may lean toward code 100 track, as it is usually the least expensive, most readily available, and sturdy. The downside is that if you compare its .100" height to the height of prototype rail, it represents rail that is used only on the most heavily trafficked main lines. Code 83 rail is a good match for 132-pounds-per-yard prototype rail, which is common on railroads that frequently ran long trains comprising cars heavily loaded with coal, crushed rock, and other

weighty commodities.

The part of the NKP that I model had a lot of 90- to 112-pound rail, so I opted for code 70 track. Most of the main line is therefore Micro Engineering flextrack, and a lot of yard and industry turnouts are their no. 6s. I used a mix of handlaid, Shinohara, and Central Valley no. 8 turnouts on the main. Sidings used lighter rail, which I modeled using ME's code 55 flextrack, although that isn't available at this writing.

If I were modeling a barely-scraping-by short line or maybe a logging railroad, code 55 rail might even be too heavy. Code 40 rail is available, but that rapidly ventures into handlaid or custom-built track territory. FastTracks makes jigs that speed up handlaid turnout and crossing

construction, and several companies will build turnouts and crossings to match your specific needs.

Wheels

There are four types of wheels you should be aware of: "hi-rail" or "tinplate," RP25, semi-scale, and fine-scale.

Toy trains and even some highly accurate scale models are equipped with wheels that have grossly oversize flanges. Some European models also have what North American modelers regard as overly deep and sharp flanges. Associated Hobby Manufacturers (no longer in business) used to import Rivarossi models that had such flanges, although current Rivarossi products have RP25 wheels.

Most models on the market today

15

Opening up a wall allows access on both sides of the Hinton, W.Va., yard and engine terminal on Ted Pamperin's HO Chesapeake & Ohio. The general yardmaster (Henry Freeman in red shirt) and roundhouse foreman/hostler work from the operator's alcove outside the layout room. The east- and west-end yardmasters (that's Ted in the blue shirt) switch from the main layout aisle.
David Olesen

have RP25 wheels, which means they are manufactured to meet Recommended Practice 25 (not a standard!) issued by the National Model Railroad Association (nmra.org). Similarly, almost all commercial track is manufactured to accommodate RP25 wheels.

So-called semi-scale wheels, available from an increasing number of manufacturers in HO scale, are known as code 88 wheels, as they are .088" wide, **11**, as opposed to RP25's .110" width. The flanges are also shallower and therefore look better, especially on tank cars and hoppers where the wheels are readily visible.

Theoretically, the narrower code 88 wheels should drop into the flangeways at frogs designed for RP25 wheels. But in my experience the more scale-like

wheels are not a problem as long as they are mounted in truck sideframes that are molded in one piece along with the connecting bolster, **11**. That is, the wheelsets are not "equalized" or free to pivot with the sideframe around the bolster. Instead, the rigid truck frame supports the code 88 wheels as they pass over the flangeways in frogs.

That said, I would venture away from using RP25 wheelsets only with due caution, as they provide excellent performance.

A small number of modelers use wheels that are shaped to match the prototype. They are known as fine-scale wheels, and the resulting models are designated Proto:87 (HO fine-scale), Proto:48 (O fine-scale), and so on. This is most advantageous in O scale, as the traditional track gauge for ¼"-scale

models is 1¼"—5 feet between the rails rather than the correct 4'-8½". The gauge error is relatively small but certainly noticeable to the discerning modeler, especially when combined with fine-scale wheels, **12**.

I won't delve deeply into the popular large scale models, which are based on a track gauge of 45mm. Their primary use is outdoors in "garden railways," but large scale indoor layouts are increasingly common, **13**. Be aware that the correct proportion for this gauge when it is treated as standard gauge is 1:32, or ⅜" scale. Many commercial models are made to 1:29 so they appear more massive, which means the rails are now somewhat too close together for scale. When a layout is built close to eye level, however, the gauge error is harder to discern.

16
Layout planners need to allow for "desk jobs" such as a dispatcher, operator(s), and yard clerk when allocating space for the railroad as a whole. My workbench serves as the Charleston, Ill., operator's desk during operating sessions, forcing me to clean it up each month.

The reach-in dilemma

I've already discussed the perennial problem with 4 x 8 layouts: They're too wide to enable you to reach the back from the front. But that same concern raises its ugly head on any model railroad where the benchwork is more than about 30" deep.

At Frankfort, Ind., on my Nickel Plate layout, for example, there were both eastbound and westbound classification yards. Not surprisingly, they were located roughly north and south of each other on either side of the main line. Since I'm doing my best to faithfully model both the look and operation of Frankfort as a Layout Design Element, my westbound yard is against the backdrop while the eastbound yard is along the aisle, **14**. Guess which one is easier to operate.

I provided a raised ledge along the fascia to make it easier to reach

17
To give conductors a place to create switch lists from a stack of waybills, Dan Holbrook built desks under the benchwork that resemble those in Burlington Northern cabooses. Note the lamp and phone. *Dan Holbrook*

Sewell, W.Va., buried deep in the Appalachians, is where the narrow-gauge Mann's Creek delivered coal for coking and for fuel to the Chesapeake & Ohio. Ted Pamperin initially planned to focus solely on MC operations but then decided to divide the layout area between it and the C&O for more operating flexibility and intensity. *Ted Pamperin*

in to uncouple cars in the westbound yard, but those who regularly switch this yard have suggested that some provision for remote uncoupling would be nice. I'm not a fan of permanent magnets glued between the rails—they're unsightly and seem to work just as well when I don't want to uncouple cars as when I do. And I had the yard finished before it occurred to me that I probably should have fitted hidden electromagnetic uncouplers during the construction phase. The jury is still out on this one, but it is a good example of how strictly adhering to the prototype may create operational problems.

Ted Pamperin got around similar concerns on his World War II depiction of the Chesapeake & Ohio's sprawling yard and engine terminal at Hinton, W.Va. The yard abutted a wall between the railroad room and

workshop, so he cut a large portal in it to allow access to the yard from both sides, **15**. The engine-terminal hostler works from the workshop area, as does the general yardmaster, who oversees the work of east- and west-end yardmasters.

Crew comforts

I used to be a big fan of crew lounges where off-duty crews could go to relax between runs while getting out of the way of on-duty crews. The former family room served as a comfortable crew lounge on the Allegheny Midland.

That floor space was deemed too valuable for railroad usage to devote to creature comforts when the NKP was designed. Moreover, I had by then discovered that crews tended to get a bit too comfortable in the lounge, and it was hard to get them to keep

checking the crew callboard for open assignments.

But there are space requirements for people that we ignore at our peril. For example, traffic is managed on my NKP by a dispatcher and two operators. Road crews talk to the operators, not the dispatcher, and the operators are responsible for OSing (reporting the passage of) trains as well as copying and posting train orders and messages. Obviously, all three need desks at which to work.

My railroad is an around-the-walls design with a central peninsula (see the December 2014 *Model Railroader*). The turnback curve at the end of the peninsula (a "blob," to use an apt term coined by track-planning guru John Armstrong) is an ideal location for the dispatcher. The operator at Frankfort, Ind. (who also handles Linden, Ind.,

As each car is sorted into a track temporarily assigned to a specific destination, the car's waybill is similarly sorted into a bill box on the fascia on my steam-era railroad. The yardmaster therefore knows the order of the cars on each track and doesn't need to "walk between the rows of cars," even visually, to switch out a specific car.

and Metcalf and Humrick, Ill.), is located at the far end of one aisle. The operator for Charleston, Ill. (who also handles Cayuga and Veedersburg, Ind., and Oakland, Ill.), resides at my workbench in the utility room, **16**.

The Allegheny Midland was controlled by a dispatcher seated at a Union Switch & Signal CTC machine, so no space was needed for operators.

Professional BNSF yardmaster Dan Holbrook has provided desks located in what look like corners of cabooses, **17**. These provide a place for road conductors to sit down and covert stacks of waybills into switch lists, a clever idea I plan to borrow for the NKP.

Time is money
Like the spectrum of choices between prototype modeling and anything-goes

freelancing, you have a wide range of options when it comes to layout planning and construction. You can go it alone, enlist a little help from your friends, or outsource some or all of the layout's design and even its construction.

The more you put into a given project, the more you usually get out of it. But if what you receive is a big dose of frustration, you'll find other ways to spend your leisure time and disposable income. Fortunately, there are a number of competent modelers who can help with any or all phases of layout design and construction right up to supplying a turn-key model railroad. (See Chapter 9's "Layout design help" on page 80.)

The main learning point here is that you can job out those tasks that you

don't enjoy doing or that require tools and skills you don't now possess.

Ready-to-use models
Back in the days when locomotive and car kits largely comprised metal castings, stamped-metal shapes, and wood or even cardstock car sides, there was quite a hue and cry as plastic models were introduced.

We hear the same thing today about ready-to-run cars and locomotives and built-up structures: "They'll be the ruination of the hobby." Nonsense!

Take a well-detailed open hopper car, for example. Someone who has a basement-size layout depicting Appalachian coal railroading will need several hundred hopper cars. He or she has a choice: Buy the higher-priced but exquisitely detailed ready-to-run

An arriving eastbound freight eases into the eastbound yard's Track E2 in Frankfort, Ind., on my HO railroad. The waiting 0-8-0 will first cut off the caboose and put it on the nearby caboose track for later transfer to the westbound yard's caboose track for its trip back west, then sort the cars into the appropriate yard tracks.

models or buy cheaper kits (if they're even available) and spend time building them that might be better devoted to building the railroad.

So the real concern here is whether you see yourself as primarily a model builder who happens to build railroad models or as a someone who is fascinated by the mechanics of operating a railroad and needs the models—the chess pieces, if you will—to make that possible.

My main goal was and is to have a realistically operating model railroad that looked every bit as realistic as it operated. Since I tend to work on the layout alone—I got more than enough of managing people at my day job before I retired, thank you—and since I'm not getting any younger, I need to find ways to get more done in less

time. (Almost) ready-to-run cars and locomotives with better detail than I could apply are therefore a boon.

Even though I have done most, but not all, of the work on both the Allegheny Midland and now the Nickel Plate by myself, I listened to my good friend Bill Darnaby when he made it very clear that I could not accomplish my goals—which were to emulate what he had done in his basement—on a single-deck railroad.

When I protested that I wasn't all that fond of multi-deck layouts, he admitted that he wasn't, either. "But I like what they let me do," he concluded. Bingo! Reality sunk in with a vengeance. Multi-deck it would be, and I turned to my good friend Frank Hodina when it came time to fit a long main line in my available space.

He wasn't saddled with the single-deck baggage I had left over from my previous layout.

You'll be faced with similar hard-nosed choices: You would like to do something, but some people you respect suggest otherwise. If you think timetable and train-order operation looks interesting, for example, I will advise you to find a single-track railroad; a double-track main takes away much of the challenge as trains tend to follow the leader.

Ted Pamperin ran squarely into that very dilemma as he planned his World War II-era Chesapeake & Ohio layout. He enjoys TT&TO operation, but he wanted to model the heavy wartime traffic through West Virginia's New River Gorge. As on the prototype, the extreme traffic density

21

Yard crews are asked to watch for and flag cars with defects such as low couplers, missing brake wheels or grab irons, or poor-rolling trucks. They then fill out Bad Order slips and switch the cars with defects onto a RIP (repair in place) track for maintenance between sessions.

could not be accommodated over a single-track main. So he weighed the stunning scenery of the central Appalachians and his great admiration for the C&O and connecting narrow gauge Mann's Creek, **18**, against the somewhat less-challenging TT&TO operations. Ted decided to stick to his guns rather than find a single-track section of the C&O to model. He's happy with his choices.

Yard design

It would take an entire book to give you even a high-level overview of yard design and operation, and fortunately for all of us, Andy Sperandeo wrote it: *The Model Railroader's Guide to Freight Yards* (Kalmbach, 2004). I also included a chapter on classification, staging, and fiddle yard design in my book, *Realistic Model Railroad Operation, Second Edition* (Kalmbach, 2014).

22

Like including a RIP track in the yard, providing a clean-out track where cars are thoroughly cleaned between loads adds an interim destination to cars and hence serves as another industry. For example, boxcars loaded with soybeans were hard to completely empty. So after unloading at the soybean plant in Frankfort, Ind., they were spotted on a track where a laborer could sweep up any remaining beans and sell them back to the bean plant.

The main thing to keep in mind when you add a yard to your railroad is that its primary function is to sort—not store—cars into logical blocks for trains that will be leaving the yard. This is much easier if you keep track of the cars as they enter the yard, putting all cars for Town A or for Division B and beyond on specific tracks. Then you can group the cars in town order and send them out on the daily local (also known as a way freight, peddler, patrol, etc.), or you can block them into a through or fast freight for delivery to the next major yard or beyond.

If you use waybills that specify the destination of each car and perhaps its lading, it helps to have a bill box for each track, **19**. As the yardmaster sorts cars, he or she can sort their waybills and place them in the appropriate track box. Each track, and associated bill box, should be assigned to cars for a (often temporary) specific destination.

For any but the smallest yards, you'll want an arrival track or open yard track or two where inbound trains can be held until they can be switched by a yard crew, **20**. Similarly, you'll want at least one departure track where blocks of cars assembled into a train are held until departure.

To avoid having the yard engine get in the way of arriving and departing freights, you'll need a yard lead that's long enough to accommodate a reasonable number of cars as they are being switched. It need not be as long as the longest train or yard track, however, as long cuts could be difficult to handle safely in pre-radio days.

The yard should have at least one readily accessible track where cabooses can be stored between runs. It should have a repair-in-place (RIP) track where cars with minor problems can be repaired. Think of this as another industry on your railroad, as cars of all types can be switched into and picked up from a RIP track. I have my crews place cars with actual defects, such as a low coupler, on the RIP track accompanied by an explanatory Bad Order slip so I can repair them between operating sessions, **21**.

It's also a good idea to include a clean-out track where cars with rem-

23 Rick De Candido's entire apartment-sized "layout" comprises a busy engine terminal and head-end-car servicing area. It's fed by staging yards and can be rolled out of the way between sessions. *Rick De Candido*

nants of a previous load, **22**, or the bracing that secured it are cleaned and prepared for their next assignments. Like the RIP track, it's another "universal industry."

Yards almost always have nearby engine terminals to service both yard and road locomotives. You'll find Marty McGuirk's book, *Model Railroader's Guide to Locomotive Servicing Terminals* (Kalmbach, 2002), helpful in this regard. As always, I highly recommend you find a prototype engine facility of the type your railroad requires and do

your very best job of plagiarizing it as a Layout Design Element (LDE).

Apartment-dwelling modeler Rick De Candido built a "layout" that accommodates the action found in a steam-era engine terminal, **23**, as he described in *Model Railroad Planning 2015*. It's mounted on casters so it can be rolled out of the way between operating sessions, and it's fed by two staging elevators—one for locomotives, the other for passenger-train equipment—that can be raised with a car jack.

1

CHAPTER THREE

Understanding railroad operations

By scaling down and selectively compressing actual prototype locations such as towns, yards, engine terminals, and industries, track planning is made easier, and the railroad will support realistic operation if that is—or later becomes—an objective. This photo shows the east end of Cayuga, Ind., my 1950s hometown. Every track that existed here has been included on the model, albeit foreshortened. I wondered why there were so many storage tracks—until I discovered I needed them to store boxcars for grain loading here and at towns farther west along the St. Louis Division.

Whether or not you now profess an interest in operating your model railroad in a manner that emulates how the full-size railroads earned their keep, it's a good idea to plan it so as to accommodate realistic operation. Interests change as our knowledge base broadens and circle of modeling friends widens, and it often pays handsomely to design and build a model railroad that will support your newfound interests, **1**. It doesn't cost anything other than doing some homework, and a better track plan almost always results from paying close attention to how full-size railroads operate.

2 How could a Burlington Northern bulkhead flatcar show up on the team track at New Sharon, Maine, on Mike Confalone's prototype-based freelanced Allagash Ry., without a series of connections between the two railroads? That's why staging or fiddle yards that simulate the rest of the North American rail network are critical components of realistic operation. The waybill in the box notes that the dimensional lumber came from Simpson Timber in Shelton, Wash. Routing: BN-Chicago-Conrail-Rotterdam Jct.-B&M-Portland-MEC-Kennebec Jct.-Allagash. *Mike Confalone*

Connecting to the rail network

One of the most important advances in model railroad design occurred when modelers quit running their trains in endless circles and began to think about how a Burlington Northern center-beam bulkhead flat car wound up on a model railroad clearly set in the Northeast, **2**.

The obvious conclusion is that it was interchanged from the originating railroad to an intermediate common carrier or two before being handed over to the railroad that would deliver the car to its consignee (receiving customer).

If, for example, a Union Pacific boxcar were loaded with lumber in Washington and consigned to a lumberyard in a Boston suburb, it probably would travel over the UP to Omaha, Neb., where it would be interchanged with the connecting Chicago & North

Western (which today is part of the sprawling UP system). The C&NW would haul it to Chicago, where it might be interchanged to the New York Central. The NYC would forward it to Albany and turn it over to subsidiary Boston & Albany for the final leg to the Boston area.

So if your railroad depicts part of the B&A or maybe is a freelanced railroad called the Boston & Western (B&W) that connects Albany with Boston, you would route the car UP-C&NW-NYC-B&A (or -B&W). If you're modeling today's railroading, the routing might be UP-CSX or UP-NS. One of the colorful New England smaller, now regional, railroads might be in the mix, **3**.

Off-stage accommodations

What all of this routing stuff implies is that your planning should include

one or more off-stage, often-hidden yards, **4**. These are where trains coming from, for example, the west to the small segment of the rail network that you've chosen to model can be staged until they're needed. Similarly, trains coming from the east need a place in which to disappear after they originate on or traverse your railroad.

The term "staging" is used to imply a passive system in which you prepare—stage—inbound trains between operating sessions. One staging yard will suffice if you have modeled a terminal yard or the end of a branch or short line. If instead your railroad is in the middle of a longer mainline run, then you'll need a staging yard at both ends of the modeled segment.

You can follow Jim Six's example, **2-7**, and connect the two staging yards so that one yard does double-duty,

3 The Green Mountain and Vermont railroads picked up where the Rutland left off. Viewed from the highway overpass, ex-Rutland Alco RS-1 405 and a switcher work near Howe Scale (now a retail complex) in Rutland, Vt., in 1972.

serving both ends of the main line while also allowing continuous running if desired.

And you can get even more mileage out of this combined yard by adding scenery and assigning a yard crew there, as Jim did, to work it in real time. Or you can locate it behind some sort of view block, perhaps in a separate room or walled-off area, and treat it as a "fiddle" yard.

A fiddle yard is simply a hidden but active yard operated by an unseen crewmember—"Pay no attention to the man behind the curtain!" This allows operating sessions of any length, as the railroad doesn't have to be restaged. Like most staging yards, fiddle yards are usually not scenicked, **5**, as they are purposefully kept out of view to support the illusion of trains coming from and going to distant locales.

The staging yards on the Allegheny Midland were and the Nickel Plate are all of a stub-ended, or "muzzle-loading," design. This saves

considerable space, as no return loop is required. Between operating sessions, trains are backed out of staging and the locomotives and cabooses are swapped by hand.

After cycling the waybills to show each car's next destination, I re-block the freight trains by hand to group cars for like destinations together, thus easing the yard crews' switching chores. The locomotive and cars that comprise the two passenger trains are also rearranged—baggage and Railway Post Office (RPO) cars, coaches, diner, and sleepers—by hand.

Since most freight trains have to be re-blocked anyway, the effort to back them out of staging and then back in again requires no more effort than if I had included a turnback loop for each end of the railroad. The only advantage of having a loop-type staging yard is for passenger trains and when entire freight trains are reused during a session. This is practical if your railroad operates a lot of look-alike commuter

trains or unit trains made up of identical "closed" cars such as tank cars, modern auto racks, container well cars, or piggyback flats.

If it's equipped with automated circuitry to change the polarity and reverse the switch, a return-loop design also supports continuous running when guests are watching the railroad go through its paces.

Managing train movements

On a one-train-a-day short line, there is no need for a dispatcher, let alone an operator. Train orders or track warrants, as described in my *Realistic Model Railroad Operations* book, can be written out ahead of time or issued orally during the session—or not even used. Here the emphasis would not be on interactions between trains but rather on switching online industries and interchanges, **6**.

Centralized Traffic Control (CTC) is a system whereby the dispatcher sits in front of a "machine"—a computer console today—and controls train movements remotely via signals and power switches, **7**. The work performed by a model railroad's dispatcher is exactly the same as that done by his or her professional counterpart, albeit without any property or lives being at risk.

The train crews also operate in an extremely realistic environment. As on the prototype, CTC accommodates a high traffic density over a single-track main line.

The potential downside is that the dispatcher, not the train crews, makes the go-no go decisions. If Simon says stop with a red signal, they wait for it to clear. This is dramatically different from a timetable and train-order environment in which the decisions about whether to move on down the line are made by the train crew based on their superiority or lack thereof,

4

The west-end staging yard on my HO railroad is 68.5" off the floor and hence hidden from ready view by a low fascia, yet easily accessed if needed. This 12-track yard accommodates all Nickel Plate trains coming from or headed toward southern Illinois and the St. Louis area.

5

Lee Nicholas's Utah Colorado Western employs a "mole"—here John Dulaney—who works an active fiddle yard located in a room away from the main railroad room. He moves cars and locos on and off the railroad during an operating session, thus allowing the railroad to operate indefinitely without restaging. Each drawer can hold the consist of a train, allowing it to be blocked ahead of time. *Lee Nicholas*

Custom layout builder Lance Mindheim switched from modeling the Monon in N scale to a simpler HO layout based on CSX's Downtown Spur in Miami, Fla. Lance enjoys the slower pace and the smaller crew requirements that this type of modern railroading affords. *Lance Mindheim*

Allen McClelland designed the HO Virginian & Ohio to be dispatched by Centralized Traffic Control, as Steve King is doing on the original hardwired CTC panel. Subsequent panels were computer based using hardware and software created by Gerry Albers. *Allen McClelland*

the timetable schedule, and any amendments issued to them in the form of train orders by the dispatcher.

CTC also requires a significant investment in some type of machine and lineside signals. You can have an authentic CTC machine custom built by CTC Components (ctccomponents@comcast.net), and several computer-based versions are available. And those signals add a great deal of visual interest and authenticity to a model railroad!

Track warrants are essentially train orders with training wheels bolted on, **8.** On prototype railroads, operator jobs were eliminated once radio communications between dispatchers and train crews became reliable. So an easier-to-use form with almost all necessary instructions already printed on it was created wherein the conductor fills in a few blanks and reads the warrant back to the dispatcher as a crosscheck.

Track warrants work equally well on a model railroad with radio communications, but there are a couple of caveats to keep in mind: First, wearing a radio headset can be uncomfortable, especially on a busy railroad with lots of radio chatter. And a train has to stop at the end of its clearance limit to copy a new warrant.

Modeling jobs

Your planning must consider the likelihood of the resulting railroad being able to attract other modelers within a reasonable driving distance if regular operating sessions are an objective. "If you build it, they will come" certainly applies to a well-designed and smoothly operating model railroad; some of my regular crewmembers drive more than two hours each way for my monthly operating sessions.

If you're a lone wolf by desire or geographical circumstance, the planning requirements change dramatically. You would then play all roles: engineer, conductor, dispatcher, station agent-operator, yardmaster, and so on.

As the size and complexity of a model railroad escalate, the need for more operators grows accordingly. My railroad requires 18 to 20 crewmembers to operate (see "Crewing the NKP" at right). Since I live in a relative hotbed of model railroad activity (northwestern New Jersey, eastern Pennsylvania, and the greater New York metropolitan area), rounding up crews for once-a-month, Sunday-afternoon operating sessions is usually not a problem.

The learning points here are two-fold: Base your railroad's design on the number of operators you're both comfortable with and believe you can count on. But don't underestimate the number of operators who may come out of the woods once word of a fun-to-operate model railroad gets around.

Operating your railroad

Railroads that operate regularly tend to operate better. Like any machine, sitting idle is not conducive to reliable

Crewing the Nickel Plate

It requires 18 to 20 crewmembers (not including me) to operate my HO scale model railroad, which depicts the Third Subdivision of the Nickel Plate Road's St. Louis line in 1954:

Chief dispatcher: Oversees the train dispatcher and coordinates with the yardmasters to anticipate the need for extra trains or sections; ensures that all trains have crews.

Dispatcher: Manages the safe and efficient operation of the subdivision by issuing train orders and messages that amend the published schedule.

Frankfort Operator: Copies train orders as required for the four towns in one main aisle; sets train-order signals; OSs (reports the passage of) trains for the four towns he represents (train crews seldom talk directly with the dispatcher); operates the small CTC machine that controls the NKP-Monon interlocking at Linden, Ind.

Charleston operator: Handles train orders and messages and OSs trains for the four towns in the second main aisle. (Operators are in effect dispatcher trainees.)

Frankfort General Yardmaster: Coordinates the functions of the east- and westbound yards; consults with the Chief Dispatcher concerning extra trains or sections needed to keep the yards fluid; alerts the east- and westbound yardmasters concerning the imminent arrival or departure of trains.

Frankfort Westbound Yardmaster: Switches all inbound westward trains and blocks trains departing Frankfort on the Peoria (staged) and St. Louis (modeled) divisions.

Frankfort Eastbound Yardmaster: Switches all inbound eastward trains and blocks eastward trains departing Frankfort over the Toledo and Sandusky divisions (both staged).

Frankfort Swing Yardmaster: Makes cross-yard moves between the EB and WB yards (cabooses are assigned to a specific division, so a caboose arriving in the EB yard off the Third Sub must be cross-yarded to head back west) and assists the other yardmasters as required.

Frankfort Roundhouse Foreman: Responsible for servicing and turning all inbound engines and assigning the proper type of locomotive(s) to all outbound trains departing over four divisions (two all-steam and two all-diesel).

Frankfort Commercial Engine: This crew switches local industries, interchanges, and the engine-supply facilities.

Frankfort Bean Plant Job: Switches the Swift soybean plant, which requires weighing all loaded and unloaded cars, moving emptied boxcars to the clean-out track, etc.

Charleston Yardmaster: Switches all through trains by removing "propers" for Charleston and "shorts" from eastbounds for delivery between Charleston and Frankfort; and adding "through" cars to through and fast (symbol) freights to fill out tonnage.

Charleston Roundhouse Foreman: Responsible for servicing and turning all inbound engines and assigning the proper type of locomotive to all outbound trains. Also works with the yardmaster to switch local industries and operate the 12-track Fourth Subdivision staging yard.

Road crews: When available, two-person crews—conductor and engineer—are assigned to all road trains, thus helping to avoid mistakes and providing a means for someone not experienced in timetable and train-order operations to "learn the ropes" from a more experienced crewmember.

Track warrants are akin to simplified train orders, as almost all needed instruction options are printed on the form; just check and confirm the appropriate box(es). This expedient allows train crews to receive instructions directly from the dispatcher by radio rather than in written form from operators in depots or towers. *Jim Providenza*

Place-location signs aren't just to help passengers know where to get off the train. They're important markers for operating crews as they observe timetable schedules or follow message, train order, or track warrant instructions.

performance. Moreover, inviting interested friends over to help you run the railroad will uncover all sorts of glitches that may have escaped your attention, or that you had gradually come to ignore: "normalization of deviation," in NASA-speak.

But be a bit selective on what advice you choose to accept. For reasons that remain unclear, the Nickel Plate did not provide a crossover in a central location that would have created a much shorter path between the engine terminal and the west end of the westbound yard. As the railroad segued into regular operation, road crews quickly spotted that deficiency and recommended that I install the "missing" crossover.

"No can do," I repeatedly replied, as the NKP didn't have one there. I am, after all, modeling a specific prototype at a specific time and place.

But is it possible to be too prototypical? Certainly. Professional railroaders did roughly the same jobs day in and day out, and we can't expect our once-a-month operating crews to develop the same degree of expertise and familiarity. So some complex tasks may need to be simplified to some degree.

But avoid dumbing things down just because some of the troops don't know how to do something and therefore protest they're "not interested" in this or that. If you overly simplify a key aspect of the environment you want to re-create in miniature—timetable and train-order operation being an excellent example—you may win the battle and lose the war. Look not to capitulation but rather education as the solution.

Get it running!

Some of us like to build a model railroad in phases, finishing each before moving on—first the benchwork, then the backdrop, then the wiring, then all trackwork, etc. Others like to avoid the tedium of repetition by doing some of this, then some of that.

However you approach your next layout's design and construction, many experienced modelers recommend that you find a way to get some significant part of it—maybe one small town fed by a staging yard—operational as rapidly as possible. That's akin to beta-testing, and it is the only way you're going to find out what you're not doing as well as you could or should. You need to learn how to improve your methodology before embarking on the rest of the journey.

Make it a goal to host regular operating sessions at the earliest possible juncture, even if you're the only one doing the operating. You'll quickly find a locomotive that derails, shorts out, operates poorly, won't haul enough tonnage, or surges going downgrade.

You may discover that a key type of locomotive runs well but simply won't do the required job—haul the desired number cars up a certain grade or negotiate a curve of the planned minimum radius. You—or, more likely, your crew—will find trackwork that gives you or them fits, and discovering what caused that will make it possible to avoid repeating the same mistake, be it the product you installed or the way you installed it.

Make a business decision

When neophytes first confront the concept of moving cars and trains in a realistic manner—that is, in a way that emulates prototype railroading—they will encounter a plethora of ways to accomplish that aim. At that point, it's easy to begin to think of realistic operation as some sort of game.

I prefer the term "simulation." We're trying to build and operate highly functional and realistic, if considerable smaller, trains. We may not climb into the cab like we could do if we were operating a flight simulator. But in all other respects realistic operation involves trying to model the more appealing aspects of working on a railroad in a manner that a professional railroader would recognize and embrace.

To that end, when one of my crewmembers asks me what to do in a given situation, I either cite an operating rule that appears in the NKP's book of rules or timetable special instructions, or I recommend that he or she "make a business decision." Rather than following some made-up game rules, it's easier and better to ask yourself what you would do if this were happening on a full-size railroad.

Would you add a gondola of scrap to a hot symbol freight just because it happens to be headed in the same direction? Would you delay that hotshot for ten minutes to allow the yard crew to tack on a cut of freshly iced meat reefers or auto parts? What would upper management prefer that you do? How about the customer (consignee)?

The Virginian did not shirk when it came time to order big, powerful locomotives from 2-8-8-2 Mallets and 2-6-6-6 Blue Ridge articulateds to 2400-hp Fairbanks-Morse Train Masters. The latter were inherited by the Norfolk & Western in the 1959 merger. The V&O followed the VGN's example with its own modest fleet of the big TMs. *V&O: Jim Boyd*

A Form 19 train order is typically used to create extras or sections or to help an inferior train move against a superior train. Here the order authorizes the movement of engine 701 "seven naught one" westward between the end points of the NKP's Third Subdivision of the St. Louis Division.

1

CHAPTER FOUR

Considerations of time

Do you see the ringers in the above photo? I model the autumn grain rush in 1954 when two of the four divisions radiating out of Frankfort, Ind., were dieselized. But the NKP didn't acquire EMD GP30s like 900 and 909 until 1962, long after the last steam locomotive's fires had been dropped. Whether such anachronisms are bothersome is a highly personal decision. But by tightly defining the modeled era, one can restrict acquisitions to that time frame, thus potentially saving money.

The idea of trying to determine where your railroad-to-be resides not only in space but also in time may seem to be a bit esoteric at this point. Your limited knowledge of prototype railroading may make it difficult if not impossible to make narrowly defined choices when it comes to selecting models.

2

Yosemite Valley modeler Jack Burgess has narrowed the modeled time frame down to August 1939. But determining exactly how things looked then has proven problematic. The first two models he built of the tower at the YV-Santa Fe crossing were painted tan with dark brown trim per a color photo. He built a third model (don't ask) and was about to repeat the color scheme when a local modeler remembered a photo in Jack's collection that suggested it was painted in AT&SF red with green trim. More research confirmed that scheme for the year Jack models. Why it was later repainted in standard Southern Pacific colors remains a mystery. *Jack Burgess*

Indeed, you may like models that represent a wide range of eras and don't want to be restricted by some nitpicker's clarion call to mind your timeline. But tightly defining a modeled era actually can lower your costs if you restrict purchases to models bounded by those time constraints, **1**.

Why model a specific period?

As you start to acquire models to populate the railroad you are planning, it may help to have already chosen a specific year or short range of years for your railroad to depict. Yes, this does restrict your choices, but it also precludes spending money on models that, despite their aesthetic appeal, don't fall within the bookends of time you have selected.

Some modelers never worry about modeling a specific period. If they like it and can afford it, they buy it. But many of us begin to zero in on a time and place that has special appeal to us. That's helpful in many ways beyond

limiting our purchases. It gives us a well-defined objective, and it provides a yardstick with which to measure the success of what we're doing. If we're modeling the Anytime & Everytime, there is no way to judge goals against accomplishments.

"Eureka!" moments

It helps to have or develop an interest in history and industrial archeology when you're planning a model railroad. That converts what could be viewed as "homework" into a series of Eureka! moments as we find yet another missing puzzle piece in the overall picture of a time and place we are striving to assemble.

Determining what goes where in a temporal sense can be difficult, and sometimes what we discover isn't all that conducive to elation. Jack Burgess is modeling California's long-gone Yosemite Valley as it existed in August 1939, and I recall him telling me about painting the tower that guarded the

YV-Santa Fe crossing. He went with his best guess based on black-and-white photos and other evidence, only to later discover that the building was indeed painted that color—but not in 1939, **2**.

There are many sources of information about prototype railroading, but focus first on the more "perishable" ones. Talking to the professionals who ran or run the segment of railroad you're modeling is well worth the time and effort, but for most "fallen flags" (abandoned or merged railroads), their numbers are dwindling.

Retired Nickel Plate (then Norfolk & Western and finally Norfolk Southern) engineer Don Daily, **3**, my chief source of information about the NKP lines out of Frankfort, Ind., and a long-time personal friend, recently passed away. Without Don's memory and archives, my representation of that part of the Nickel Plate would have been much less faithful to the prototype. Fortunately, Don was very

gracious about sharing information and his time. Those who didn't have the same opportunity to know him would face a much more difficult challenge when gathering information for a similar model railroad. Or, put in a more positive light, it's now my turn to pass along what Don taught me.

Joining a railroad-specific historical society is almost always an excellent investment. Some have modeling departments associated with them, sometimes in their printed periodical or online, available to all or just to members. An internet search will usually point you to a group devoted to documenting the history of even the most obscure railroad. It's only fair that you support them financially if you are to benefit from their work.

Books and films on DVDs also provide clues as to what is appropriate for a given era. Aerial and satellite photos are readily available online.

Maps can be especially helpful. I already mentioned U.S. Geological Survey quadrangle topographic maps.

3 Retired NKP-N&W-NS engineer Don Daily (top photo), the last fireman to break in on steam out of the NKP's Frankfort, Ind., engine terminal, was the chief advisor for my HO railroad. Interviewing railroaders and workers such as this mine tipple foreman talking to Allen McClelland, Jim Boyd, and me about his job is one of the best ways to discover how a railroad or industry really operated. *Mike Del Vecchio; Steve King*

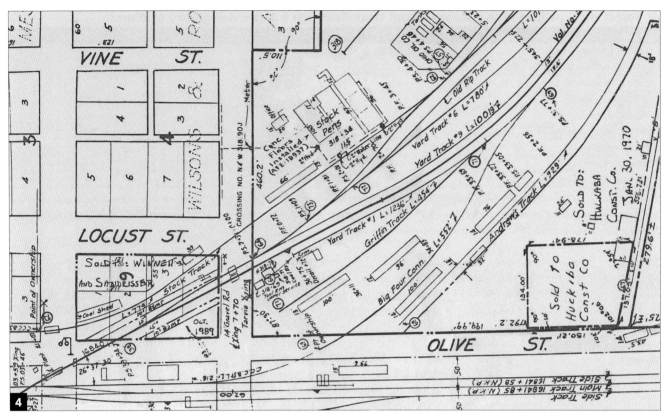

Valuation ("val") maps like this one showing the Nickel Plate-Big Four crossing in Charleston, Ill., were produced when the U.S. Government took over the railroads during World War I. These detailed scale drawings are stored at the National Archives Annex in College Park, Md. They often formed the basis for railroad right-of-way maps that have endured into modern times.

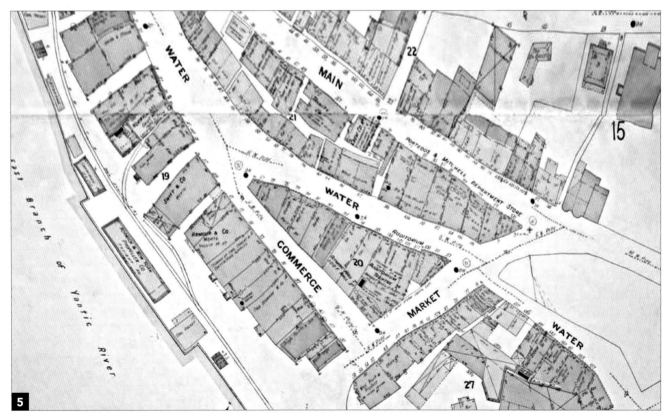

Sanborn fire insurance maps help identify the footprint, construction, and number of stories of commercial and residential structures. Track arrangements are usually approximate. Many large libraries have collections showing cities and towns.

Marty McGuirk collection

6: Selecting a period in the steam-diesel transition era for the Allegheny Midland

Event	1950	1951	1952	1953	1954	1955	1956	1957	1958	1959
NKP S/S-1 2-8-4s on Wheeling							>>>>	>>>>		
NKP I-3 2-6-6-2s in service	>>>>	>>>>	>>>>	>>>>	>>>>	>				
NKP J-1 4-8-2s in service	>>>>	>>>>	>>>>	>>>>						
NKP SD9s in service								>>>	>>>>	>>>>
NKP RSD-12s in service								>>>	>>>>	>>>>
WM steam on Elkins line	>>>>	>>>>	>>>>	>>>>	>>					
WM speed lettering						>>>	>>>>	>>>>	>>>>	>>>>
"Alphajet" fast freights						>>	>>>>	>>>>	>>>>	>>>>
Wheeling District dieselized								>	>>>>	>>>>

When backdating the Allegheny Midland, I made a table using Microsoft Word to identify ranges of key events. Railroad histories and locomotive guides identified dates when key events started or ended. My desire to use SD9s and RSD-12s alongside steam power quickly pointed to 1957 as being a good year to model.

Much more detailed maps were made by the federal government when they took over control of U.S. railroads during World War I. These valuation maps, 4 and 8-6, served as the basis for railroad right-of-way maps for decades thereafter. Many railroad historical groups have copies on file.

Another series of helpful maps was produced by the Sanborn Fire Insurance Co., 5. These show structures insured against loss by fire, with intricate keys describing the construction of the buildings and often overall footprint dimensions. They cannot be relied upon as the final word on railroad track arrangements, but they're usually pretty close. Many state, college, and even local libraries have copies.

Railroad cars have the date they were built (BLT) and the date they were reweighed (shop initials and date, which is always later than the BLT or NEW date) stenciled on them. So a car that says "BLT 3-47" with a reweigh date of 5-55 would not be appropriate for my autumn 1954 railroad. One stenciled "BLT 3-18" would also be suspect as not sufficiently up to date for a 1954 railroad.

Timeline matrix
Whether you're modeling a specific prototype or freelancing based on prototype railroads, making a timeline matrix, 6, is helpful. My simple table has columns for years and rows for various features: locomotive types, major structures, and specific trains. When it is finished, you can usually find at a glance a year or even a portion of a year when the features you want to model were in service.

If you view digging out such facts as pure drudgery, I recommend either giving it a try in the hopes of discovering that it is a lot more interesting than you may now imagine, or that you not give a second thought to locating your railroad on a narrowly defined timeline.

More subtle time hacks
As you dig into railroad and North American history, you'll find a number of "markers" that help define eras. Among them are freight cars equipped with consolidated and U-1 wheel stencils and the removal of running boards (don't call them "roofwalks"), 7; the mandate to put "ditch lights" on the pilots of locomotives; and the demise of cabooses and their replacement by end-of-train (EOT) devices.

In the 1970s, *Railroad Model Craftsman* published foldout charts prepared by Charles Buccola called RailDates. These handy references pinpointed when important events occurred as an aid to modelers who want to ensure chronological accuracy of details. Chief among them are major railroad mergers and abandonments.

You've heard of "analysis paralysis." This occurs when you fail to keep moving forward because you lack "all available" information. The quest for more data never ceases, and there

7
Steam-era boxcars got a new look when running boards were removed and ACI scanning labels (to left of door), consolidated stencils (black rectangles), and U-1 wheel stencils (black square with yellow or white dot) began to be applied in the 1970s. By this time, the era of the 40-foot boxcar was nearly over.

A shortage of good-condition boxcars in the 1970s led to incentive-per-diem cars. Most sported the reporting marks of short lines, but the cars were actually owned by investors capitalizing on the high daily rental fees. The South Branch Valley boxcar paint scheme was borrowed from my freelanced Ridgeley & Midland County HO boxcars. Model Die Casting (now part of Athearn) made kits for both cars, but the model is the prototype!

comes a point when you should go with what you have.

The 1970s boxcar craze

One remarkable period in railroad history was in the 1970s when a boxcar shortage was addressed by allowing higher daily rental fees ("incentive per diem") for certain types of boxcars, **8**. Investors made deals with short lines to use their names and reporting marks on brand new boxcars that were free to roam the North American rail network while the rental fees accumulated. When this bubble burst, as all bubbles

eventually do, those cars came home to roost. Strings of stored cars filling every unused foot of track were a common sight on many short lines.

To add a bit more color to that decade, many railroads commemorated the Nation's bicentennial in 1976 with locomotives painted in red, white, and blue paint schemes that ranged from tasteful to garish. Since Amtrak had debuted in 1971, creating a wild range of mix-and-match road names and paint schemes in passenger train consists, modeling the 1970s became popular and still warrants consideration.

Regional railroads

The 1970s also saw the debut of what become known as regional railroads. Some were simply short lines built on the bones of branches spun off by major railroads; others were truly regional in nature—simply smaller versions of mainline railroads.

Modeling a regional railroad is a popular modeling theme today. Some have taken over long segments of abandoned railroads—the Iowa Interstate hustling freight over former Rock Island lines (the Rock was abandoned in 1980) is a good example; **1-11**.

1

CHAPTER FIVE

Geography isn't generic

Even at a glance, there's little doubt that Colorado & Southern 2-8-0 No. 340 is situated deep in the Rockies on Mary and Bill Miller's On3 railroad, thanks largely to the photo backdrop. Such geographical clues depicting distinctive regional geological features are helpful to viewers. The blueprint schematic mounted on the fascia makes it easy for crews to relate waybill or switch list destinations to car spots. *Paul Dolkos*

Geography is a wonderful tool to help viewers understand where your railroad resides. I often hear modelers talking about adding "mountains and maybe a port" to their railroads, but often as not the result is a decidedly mixed message. What mountains? Which port on what ocean or lake or river? As long as you're going to the trouble of building a mountain ridge or harbor, its physical characteristics might as well tell the viewer what he or she is looking at, **1**.

Effective communication

Prototype modelers have it easy when it comes to conveying what, where, and when their railroads represent, *if* they pay attention to the details that point to specific types of railroading in readily identifiable locations and eras. Freelancers, on the other hand, must use great care to avoid confusing the audience—I assume they will be sharing their creativity with visitors or readers—with some of this and some of that and precious little to connect the two.

Communicating anything assumes a common language. The audience we most want to impress will be those who have sufficient knowledge to understand what it is we are trying to do. The "general public," which often includes close family members, may be awed by one's ability to make those tiny trains move and produce chugging sounds as they negotiate tunnels and high trestles. But it would be ever so nice if we could also measure up to the expectations of a more discerning audience: fellow modelers who have been around the block a few times.

Little things can derail big things. Parking an Edsel next to a 4-4-0 would do it unless that locomotive was operating on a tourist line. But most of us are cognizant of such hiccups. Where we more often fail is in our assumption that scenery is generic, that this mountain looks like that one. The forces that built today's mountain ranges acted in different ways on different types of bedrock, and at different times. So the roughly 10-million-year-old "pointy" Rockies, **2**, only vaguely resemble the rounded Appalachians, which have endured not one but at least two major "orogenies" over the past 400 million years or so. And one part of the Appalachians may look markedly different from another as we view metamorphic bedrock or level or tilted and folded sedimentary rocks.

When building any type of scenery, there is one word I can use to describe the ideal approach to this task: plagiarize! We wouldn't scratchbuild a boxcar or caboose or steam locomotive without photos and drawings. So why would we "scratchbuild" an entire

The Rockies are quite young as mountains go and hence still retain their steep slopes and deep valleys. At top, Rio Grande train 701 negotiates a V-shaped valley near Egeria, Colo., in June 1993. The ancient Appalachians have undergone uplift, erosion to a plain, renewed uplift, and then scraping and gouging by miles-thick ice sheets. The summits of today's Appalachians are the surface of that peneplain, as is evident in the lower photo at Hawks Nest, W.Va., along the New River. East of the bridge, the Chesapeake & Ohio (today's CSX) uses both sides of the river. *D&RGW: Chuck Conway*

3 Union Pacific 4-6-6-4 Challengers 3966 and 3964 swing through Dale Junction, Wyo., as they continue their assault of Sherman Hill on Mike Brock's HO edition of this famous stretch of railroad. The color and shape of the rock formations instantly identifies the location. *Mike Brock*

4 The grade facing Rio Grande train 177 in Glenwood Canyon in September 1977 isn't as steep as it appears; the sedimentary rocks themselves are dipping to the right. They were deposited level but then uplifted and tilted as the Rockies were elevated about ten million years ago. *Chuck Conway*

5 Grain elevators, popularly known as sentinels of the prairies, are "signature structures": They are identified with a region and attest to the local economy that fuels the railroads. Here one stands guard alongside the Burlington Northern (former Great Northern) depot at Niobe, N.D., in June 1991 *Chuck Bohi*

mountain ridge without consulting equally valid information about the "prototype"?

This probably comes under the heading of "ignorance is bliss," but that is increasingly less likely to be a safe out. The Internet has made it easy to share information and, more importantly, to obtain information. If we fail to do our due diligence on any topic, in short order we will almost certainly be duly informed of our transgressions. Of course, we can choose to keep our (however dim) light under a bushel basket, thus giving more knowledgeable modelers no opportunity to critique or praise our work, but what's the fun of that? As when doing research, sharing is ideally a big part of what a hobby offers.

Signature scenes and structures

In model railroad terminology, the word "signature" is used to mean something that is a readily recognizable characteristic of a place or structure. It can be specific—Horseshoe Curve, Sherman Hill, **3**, Cumbres Pass, Glenwood Canyon, **4**, Cincinnati Union Terminal—or a bit more generic, such as coal mines or grain elevators, **5**, the latter aptly called the sentinels of the prairies.

By carefully choosing types of scenery and structures, we can save ourselves a lot of communications work. The viewer can readily grasp what it is we are doing and where it is located. Conversely, a lack of geographical focus—a big city scene here, snow-covered peaks there, coal mines between them—may be a scenic tour de force but won't help to convey your overall message.

Regional characteristics

A friend who is building a basement-size freelanced railroad set in Tennessee asked me to comment on a novel method he had developed to make rock outcroppings, **6**. He had read some of my comments about paying attention to local geology (see *Planning Scenery for Your Model Railroad*, Kalmbach, 2007) and wanted to see whether he was heading in the right direction.

Layers of various types of sedimentary rocks may be as level as they were when deposited under an inland sea or ocean, as here on Andy Keeney's HO Nashville Road set in Tennessee, or they may have been tilted and even folded by the forces that built a mountain range. Andy made these outcroppings by stacking layers of Quikrete expansion joint material, a technique developed by his friend Bob Stevens. *Andy Keeney*

Indeed he was. A check of a geological map and photos of the rock formations in the area he is modeling showed that the rock strata were relatively level. He understood that the sedimentary rocks that were visible in one rock outcropping should match those of another nearby rock outcropping, including the coloration of the layers of different types of sedimentary rock: limestone, sandstone, shale, coal, conglomerate, and so on. With a little tweaking of the colors that differentiate between adjacent layers of rock, he was in good shape.

Look, too, at the water. Hint: It usually isn't blue unless you're looking off into the distance and actually seeing the sky reflected off of its surface. My

travels in New England told me that lots of streams and rivers there are almost transparent; one can easily see rocks lining the riverbed, **7**. Modeling such waterways with resin is therefore a good technique. But in Appalachia and the Midwestern plains, muddy water is more typical. I therefore use the same pea-soup green color that Union Switch & Signal painted their CTC machines to give my plaster-filled streambeds a base coat. I tint this with brown acrylics, add several overcoats of gloss medium, and then drybrush foam streaks downstream of piers and fallen trees with white, **8**.

Rapidly running rivers in the mountains range from opaque to crystal clear. Like most rivers, the

Animas River alongside which the Durango & Silverton runs undoubtedly changes colors with seasonal runoff. But when I last rode the D&S in the fall, the water was burdened with sediment and almost opaque. I suspect this could be modeled using plaster with painted highlights to suggest rocks just under the surface.

Bottom line: Don't automatically default to using resin. It may or may not capture the right look.

Scenery shortcuts

I suspect the three aspects of building a model railroad that most intimidate newcomers are benchwork, wiring, and scenery. We will discuss benchwork and wiring in Chapter 9, although both

7

The appearance of a stream may vary greatly depending on its location, angle of viewing, and the time of year. New England streams tend to be rocky and relatively transparent (top), whereas the typical mid-continent river—here the Kansas (Kaw) River near Topeka (center)—is often a brownish-green "CTC machine" color. Appalachian streams (bottom), here along the former Clinchfield, are often brownish-green as well. *Kaw River: Jeff Aley*

topics have been the focus of several books.

Scenery need not be a showstopper. Today, we are blessed with a multitude of products that make it relatively easy to do a credible job with basic scenery. Simply painting the subroadbed a grass or earth color and coating it with a layer of ground foam will make a world of difference.

We used to regard modeling trees as a challenge, but this is more a matter of how you approach this task than it a lack of availability of raw materials. On the Allegheny Midland, I was seldom modeling trees but rather forest canopies, **9**. In 1981, Don Cassler and I co-discovered the process that came to be known as puffball trees, and I used them to cover the verdant ridges that surrounded the railroad.

For my Nickel Plate Road HO railroad, however, I needed to model individual trees or small groves ("woods"). Scenic Express SuperTree armatures allowed me to produce a credible tree in under a minute (see the May 2014 MR). I didn't need thousands of them, as on the AM, but I still needed a surprising number of trees. That made conserving time as important as monetary cost.

Ted Pamperin is modeling the New River Gorge area of West Virginia in the late autumn of 1944. Again, SuperTrees came to the rescue, but Ted took it one additional step by inserting the tree armatures into a panel of 2" foam, taking the panel outdoors, and randomly spraying the tree armatures with a variety of hues to represent deciduous trees after the leaves have dropped off, **10**. The entire panel was then inserted into his layout. What could have been an arduous, time-consuming task became an assembly line of scenic panels that quickly covered his benchwork with realistic fall scenery.

Digital photo backdrops

One of the most important new modeling tools is the digital camera. It allows us to instantly see how well a photo turned out and make corrections on the spot. It allows us to download the photos to computers and use

8

I filled the Wabash River bed with plaster, painted it with "US&S CTC Machine Green" latex paint (which I also use for ground cover and fascias), mixed in some brown acrylic paint closer to the shore, topped it off with several coats of gloss medium, then drybrushed on white foam streaks. Beyond the bridge shadow where the blue sky reflects on the river, I added gray and then blue to the mix.

photo-editing software to remove any blemishes, make some color and exposure adjustments, add exhaust smoke or a glorious sky, crop the photo, send it to fellow modelers or a publisher, and so on.

Digital photos have also become a very popular way of producing realistic backdrops, **11.** Where we were once coached to believe that highly realistic backdrops distracted from the 3-D models, we now realize that they complement the modeling. Even professional artists have converted from painted to photographic backdrops, **12.**

A check of the ads in the model railroad magazines and a Web search will point you to several sources for such backdrops, among them SceniKing (sceniking. com) and Backdrop Warehouse (backdropwarehouse.com). Making your own photo backdrops, as Jim Six does, is not an onerous chore, but be sure the ink won't quickly fade under ultraviolet light if you use fluorescent fixtures.

9

Capturing the look of verdant Eastern forests requires modeling not individual trees but rather the forest canopy. Poly-fiber "puffball" trees coated with ground foam or leaf flakes do a fine job of achieving the desired look. The two coal tipples were intended as easily kitbashed stand-ins for specific prototype structures but developed "roots" and were never replaced.

10

To achieve the look of an Appalachian forest after the leaves have fallen, Ted Pamperin mounts Scenic Express SuperTree armatures on foam panels, then sprays them en masse with a variety of colors ranging from gray to rust. The panels are then dropped into place. *Ted Pamperin*

The majesty of the Rockies that embraced the Rio Grande Southern would be hard to model without the sense of distance and perspective that photo backdrops bring to a model railroad such as Dale Kreutzer's Sn3 (1:64, 3-foot gauge) RGS. Dale photographs his own backdrop images on site and has them printed on long rolls. *Dale Kreutzer*

Retired art teacher Tom Johnson used to hand-paint his backdrops, but now he uses digital photos that he shoots locally. He then paints the foreground scenery such as roads to match the backdrop photo. *Tom Johnson*

1

CHAPTER SIX
Plausibility

It's no longer possible to watch Yosemite Valley trains make their daily trek between Merced and the national park, unless you visit a model railroad like the one built by master modeler Jack Burgess. Jack's layout accurately reflects both the appearance and operations of the YV in August 1939. *Jack Burgess*

"How will it play in Peoria?" has long been a cautionary question that suggests we consider the audience before we unilaterally push ahead on a personal quest. Even prototype modelers are not immune to such concerns: Something as simple as a lack of weathering—often reflecting a personal preference or even a fear of failure—can preclude the degree of "everydayness" that converts a collection of nicely painted and detailed models into miniatures that can help to convince us that we are seeing Reality, not simply a model railroad. Of such subtle refinements are time machines built, **1**.

Familiarity

If something looks familiar, we tend to accept it without question. But if something looks a bit odd, we question it. That's not good when we're trying to convince the viewer that we have modeled a specific time and place.

Many modelers choose to model the extraordinary; they get plenty of the mundane in their daily lives. So they enjoy building structures that evoke the lavishly ornate structures of the late 1800s and steam locomotives that boasted multiple colors, Russia iron jacketing, and elaborate pinstriping, **2**. It's hard to argue with such efforts, as the models are extremely handsome and evoke a time when style and fashion ranked right up there with function.

But it's a bit like modeling fall foliage: A little bit goes a long way. When you model autumn foliage, the need to include a healthy dose of Ordinary doesn't go away, **3**. Indeed, the few who have done this successfully remind us to include a majority of trees still sporting green leaves and let the yellows and oranges and reds serve only as accents.

Similarly, not everything was built or painted earlier today, regardless of the era we choose to depict. One house may look like the painters just packed up and departed, but those not far away may be in need of considerable refreshment. Indeed, it's their plainness that sets off the more eye-catching structures.

One word will go a long way toward pointing you in a comfortable direction: white. White-lead paint was very durable. So most neighborhoods and farms exhibited a preponderance of white homes. Barns and farm outbuildings were often painted an earthen red because that paint was both durable and cheap, **4**.

You can't blame kit and ready-to-use structure manufacturers for producing models that will catch your eye. But that bright yellow house with blue trim can be used only once without attracting undue attention, so it pays to paint or repaint the model with good ol' white paint. The same structure with but minor alterations—perhaps

Early locomotive builders showcased their wares with elaborate bright work and striping. Don Ball models California's Stockton & Copperopolis in 1895, when spit-and-polish was the norm. Note the Russia iron boiler jacket, brass bands, and pinstriping on the Alva. *Don Ball*

My goal in modeling the fall was to take advantage of the traffic generated by moving autumn grain to market. I tried to avoid adding too much garish color to the foliage, which would have attracted one's attention to the context rather than to the action on my railroad.

removing a porch or adding a kitchen annex—can be used multiple times if it's painted white.

Weathering

Weathering models to show that they were worked hard and put away wet, or at least not painted or cleaned up recently, has long been a controversial topic. Indeed, when brass steam locomotives were first introduced, modelers often avoided painting them for fear of causing harm or even diminishing their resale value. (Residual value is the realm of the collector, not the scale modeler!)

Today, unweathered models are the exception rather than the norm for modelers who seek to convey a specific era. Obviously, every locomotive and car could not have been painted this morning, so they should show some degree of exposure to work and weather.

Fortunately, there are now easy ways to weather everything from locomotives to highway pavement, and most of them can be removed if initial efforts fail to live up to expectations.

As I explained in the November 2013 *Model Railroader,* I used a new (to modelers) product called PanPastels

4

Farmers were frugal, especially in the years following the Depression, and they used paint that was both durable and less expensive—white for the residence, barn red elsewhere. Modeling the ordinary adds realism and plausibility to a model railroad by avoiding having any one thing stand out.

5

Weathering a car or locomotive is quick and easy as long as it has a dull finish. I weathered 20 Accurail kit-built gondolas and single-sheathed boxcars in less than an hour using PanPastels from Colorfin. The foam wedge shown here is my favorite applicator.

to weather a factory-painted steam locomotive in just over seven minutes. I also weathered 12 single-sheathed wood boxcars and 8 steel gondolas, all Accurail kits that came with a flat finish, in 45 minutes, **5**.

The point isn't whether these are now contest-quality models or even examples of top-quality weathering. The goal was to quickly add 20 freight cars to the railroad's roster that did not look freshly painted. My edition of the Nickel Plate Road's St. Louis Division

requires hundreds of freight cars to function properly, and there is no way that I can spend hours, or even 45 minutes, weathering each and every car and locomotive.

Getting the graphics right

If you're modeling one of today's regional railroads, the sky is the limit where the graphic design of diesel paint schemes is concerned. Some show some artistic talent, while others are quite amateurish. You can't miss.

And many short lines are owned by one parent, **6**, so all you have to do is buy a factory-painted model for that family of railroads and make slight changes to adapt it to your freelanced railroad.

But back when diesels were just beginning to displace steam, almost all paint schemes were designed by a handful of graphic artists, most of whom worked for Electro-Motive. Former *Railfan & Railroad* editor Jim Boyd visited the EMD design studio and saw French curves (drafting aids) that had the familiar EMD curves marked on them. It was thus no accident that the same graphic elements were repeated on railroads that had no other common traits or ownership, **7**.

To a lesser extent, Alco, Baldwin, and Fairbanks-Morse similarly influenced the paint schemes on both cab and hood units. (See my book, *Realistic Model Railroad Design*, Kalmbach, 2004.)

It follows that anyone who is building a freelanced model railroad with a roster that includes EMD E and F units would be wise to carefully mimic the design elements found on prototype "covered wagons." Once again, plagiarizing is the safest approach. Every step toward individuality incurs considerable risk of venturing outside the rather confined graphic borders defined by EMD. This is actually a benefit, however, as you can buy a factory-painted model and subtly alter its paint scheme and lettering.

Two good examples of adapting common EMD graphic design elements to create new but still plausible and handsome freelanced paint schemes are evident on E units on Bill Darnaby's Maumee Route, **8**, and Mike Schafer's Illinois & St. Louis, **9**.

Using photo editing software—I use Adobe's *Photoshop Elements*—it's easy to take a digital photograph of a model or prototype locomotive and change the colors, **8**, to see which you may prefer before actually painting a model. Using PSE, just go to Enhance, scroll down to Adjust Color, then

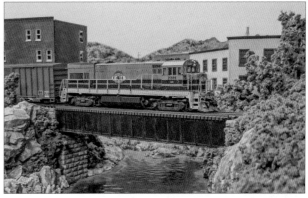

6

Genesee & Wyoming owns shortline railroads all over the world, including the St. Lawrence & Atlantic. Train 394 at Windsor, Ont., is running from Richmond, Quebec, to Lewiston Junction, Maine. Re-lettering a factory-painted G&W unit with custom decals for a mythical short line, as Richard Deuso did for his freelanced Franklin & Lamoille Railroad, is therefore highly plausible. *Richard Deuso*

over to Replace Color. In the box that shows up on the screen, go down to the Replacement area and set the tip of the eyedropper symbol on the color you want to replace and click there. Then click on the color sample you picked in the photo or slide the Hue setting to change that color to the one you want. You can tweak it a bit with the Saturation setting. You will see the color change on the image of the original photo. Of course, do this only on a copy, not the original file!

Company structure colors

Almost all railroads set standards for the appearance of their structures. This often embraced not only the colors buildings were painted but also their basic architecture, **10**. Standard plans for depots of several sizes were typical.

Simply painting a common kit-built structure in your railroad's standard paint scheme can often disguise its all-too-familiar origins and help it to blend right in, **5-15**. Simple changes to the kit's architecture may go even further to hide its common heritage.

The goal here is twofold: First, you don't want the viewer to recognize a kit and start to ponder whether you did as good a job as she did when building it. You don't want the viewer to be thinking "Fine Scale Miniatures" when you wanted them to think "West Liberty, Iowa." Second, you want the structure to more closely resemble a building in the region you are modeling for the simple reason that you chose to

7

The Atlantic Great Eastern is in every respect an excellent example of prototype-based freelancing. Jack Ozanich applied a standard EMD paint scheme similar to that used by the Lehigh Valley (note subtle striping differences) as well as the Maine Central and Boston & Maine, thus giving the railroad instant credibility. Jack operates steam when he can round up a full crew or diesels when fewer operators are available. *Craig Wilson*

model that time and place because of its attributes. Each and every structure must support those attributes and hence your central message.

I followed Chesapeake & Ohio structure standards when selecting and building structures for the Allegheny Midland, **10**, and now I model specific Nickel Plate structures, **11**. Both railroads painted their depots and lineside structures two-tone gray with a third color for doors. Shades of gray seldom lend themselves to classy-looking buildings. But they do look oh, so "railroady."

Kitbashing vs. scratchbuilding

In Chapter 8, we'll take a detailed look at various ways to obtain the structures you'll need to help people understand what they're looking at or where the freight and passenger cars are coming from and going to.

For now, let me simply note that it's important for you to understand up front how you regard the models that support your railroad vs. the models that actually move.

If building scenery and structures is an aspect of the hobby that you find to be extremely rewarding, you may want

8

The Maumee cab-unit paint scheme embodies familiar graphic-design elements from other EMD paint schemes. Using photo-editing software such as *Photoshop Elements*, it's easy to shift the burgundy to see whether a different color might be appealing. *Original (top) photo: Bill Darnaby*

9

For passenger units on the Illinois & St. Louis, a prototype-based but freelanced HO railroad, graphic designer Mike Schafer adapted common EMD styling themes to create a new yet "familiar" livery. Design themes of neighboring Rock Island plus Boston & Maine and Maine Central are evident on this E8 painted by Art Danz. *Mike Schafer*

to plan a railroad that is modest in its scope. That way, you will have time to focus on the scenery and structures.

If instead you find building scenery and structures to be little more than a time-consuming but necessary context for the railroad's operation, you may want to model sparsely settled areas and keep the benchwork narrow. But street scenes often make highly rewarding modeling projects. Kip Grant's modestly sized HO Delaware & Hudson offers good examples, **12**.

Extending the timeline

One form of prototype-based freelancing that seems to work well is to modify or extend the timeline. For example, if you're fond of the New York, Ontario & Western, which was abandoned in 1957, but also appreciate more modern equipment, you could assume that all or some portion of the O&W survived into the 1960s or beyond, **13**.

Similarly, you could assume a railroad lost through a merger somehow escaped that fate. Norfolk Southern recently opened up that door for the prototype-based freelancer by repainting GE and EMD units in paint schemes representing each of the railroads that merged to become the NS. I could acquire a small fleet of NS GEVOs factory painted in NKP livery to handle today's freight traffic, **14**. St. Louis does, after all, offer an attractive alternative to routing traffic through the perennially congested Chicago Gateway.

The bottom line

If you're modeling a specific prototype in a narrowly framed time and place, the chief task confronting you is that everything contributes to that quest. It takes only a few breaches of etiquette to diminish the overall impact of your accomplishments. The old saw that "It's my railroad, so I can do what I want" resonates only until you show it to someone else. Then the need to communicate your ideas in a pleasing and uncomplicated manner assumes a major role.

If you're freelancing but pinning your accomplishments to a particular

10 Chesapeake & Ohio's distinctive board-and-batten depots and other structures shared many architectural details. The yardmaster's office at Quinnimont, W.Va. (top) resembled a standard interlocking tower set atop a standard depot. My scratchbuilt model (above) served at Big Springs Junction on the Allegheny Midland.

11 The Nickel Plate's eastbound yard office in Frankfort, Ind., looks a lot like a depot (inset). This was the yard's operating hub and therefore deserved to be accurately modeled, an easy scratchbuilding project using Evergreen styrene siding, Pikestuff shingle panels, and Tichy and Grandt Line windows and doors.

12 Kip Grant's HO scale Delaware & Hudson, set in the fall of 1962, is a modest-size railroad (see *Great Model Railroads 2011*). This allowed Kip to devote considerable time to detailing scenes such as the downtown area of Sonnyvale, N.Y. It's well detailed but not overdone to the point of being a caricature. *Kip Grant*

railroad or region, you have an even bigger communications job ahead of you. You cannot rely on the viewer's knowledge of the prototype to complement what you're doing. Your work has to stand on its own merits.

Every step you take away from the base prototype(s) in pursuit of individualism is on increasingly soft terrain. You can sing "I did it my way!" without missing a note while utterly failing to convince anyone that you have stayed

comfortably within the bounds of Plausibility.

Is that important to you? Be sure you fully understand your answer, and how your answer is likely to change in the future, before proceeding.

Here's what a New York, Ontario & Western GE U-boat would have looked like had the O&W survived past its 1957 abandonment. Lackawanna Valley U30B 901, which began life as New York Central 2888, pauses alongside the former NYO&W headquarters and station in Middletown, N.Y., on a fan trip out of Hoboken, N.J. *Jim Odell*

Assuming that (1) the Nickel Plate Road didn't merge into the Norfolk & Western in 1964 and (2) that the NKP's St. Louis Division was therefore not abandoned, here's what it might look like today as an NKP General Electric ES44AC (an Athearn model of one of the Norfolk Southern's Heritage Fleet) and an Allegheny Midland GEVO (from Fox Valley) team up to power a freight east of Metcalf, Ill., on my HO scale NKP layout.

1

CHAPTER SEVEN

Prototype freelancing —by the prototype!

The origin of the modern Wheeling & Lake Erie's paint scheme is obvious when it's coupled next to a Rio Grande SD40T-2 "tunnel motor." Like Rio Grande units, the Wheeling scheme evolved from a small to a large road name, as is visible on the trailing unit. "Grande Gold" paint is noticeably less orange than the W&LE color. Tunnel motors were designed with radiator intakes just above the frame to pick up the lower, cooler air in Western U.S. tunnels, but several of them have migrated east after being bumped aside by newer power. This makes them fair game for freelanced Eastern railroads. *Bill Kloss*

I grew up in the Midwest, so it's natural for me to have a keen interest in granger railroading. But after a few trips to Colorado, I became a fan of the Denver & Rio Grande Western. As I photographed Rio Grande power and trains, I began to sense something familiar about them. One day it hit me: In many ways the D&RGW was a western version of my former hometown favorite, the Nickel Plate. And when the resurrected Wheeling & Lake Erie adapted the D&RGW diesel paint scheme, **1**, it became obvious that I was witnessing a form of prototype-based freelancing done by full-size railroads.

Distinctive road names

By the steam/diesel transition era, both the Denver & Rio Grande Western and the New York, Chicago & St. Louis were widely known by their nicknames: Rio Grande and Nickel Plate Road. Neither made much use of their classic heralds but rather emblazoned a stylized road name on their locomotive tenders or the flanks of their diesel fleet. Although both railroads adopted simpler versions of the original multi-stripe schemes, the basic graphic treatment remained, **2** and **3**.

Their freight-car fleets were similarly adorned not with the railroads' heralds but with stylized road names, **4**. Hoppers, gondolas, and flat cars were painted black with white lettering; boxcars were freight car brown.

Short passenger trains

Late to dieselize, the NKP never acquired covered wagons save for a modest fleet of Alco PA-1s, whereas the Rio Grande dieselized earlier with fleets of EMD F units. But both railroads did operate short passenger trains—D&RGW's *Yampa Valley Mail,* Denver to Craig, and NKP's Nos. 9 and 10, Cleveland to St. Louis—behind a single Alco PA-1, **5**. Moreover, in later years both railroad's passenger trains included distinctive Pullman-Standard-built lightweight passenger cars, **6**.

By the time the D&RGW's F units had grown long of tooth and survived only on the *Rio Grande Zephyr* in the immediate post-Amtrak years, and when NKP steam was retired in 1958 and passenger service ended in 1965, both railroads had turned their freights over to hood units. The Rio Grande had a more varied and eventually more modern roster, as the NKP merged into the Norfolk & Western before the GP40 and SD40 debuted, but watching a consist of D&RGW or NKP GP30s move freight once again pointed to the similarities despite the vastly different geographic challenges.

Which is the prototype?

My point here is that one could consider either the Rio Grande or the Nickel Plate as the prototype for a

2 An SD7-SD9 consist shows off Rio Grande's original (5308) and simplified intermediate (5302) schemes featuring black carbodies with Grande Gold lettering and striping. Note the three body stripes on the 5308 and the frame stripe on the 5302, both similar to NKP schemes. *Louis A. Marre collection*

3 Much like the Rio Grande paint scheme's evolution, NKP's hood-unit livery started with three carbody stripes but, beginning in 1959, many units were repainted in a simpler scheme with a richer yellow. Lead unit 484, a steam generator-equipped GP9 for use in passenger service, was repainted (but not recently!) in the post-1959 scheme.

freelanced model railroad that looks a lot like one, hence both, of those railroads. Despite the vastly different terrain served by the two railroads, in many ways either would serve nicely as a prototype-based freelanced version of the other.

The usual recommendation is that a prototype-based freelanced railroad should reflect not only the physical appearance of the base prototype(s) but also be located in the same general region. But, as we'll discuss in a moment, there are enough notable

Rio Grande boxcars were painted freight car brown; hoppers, gondolas, and flats were black; and all had white lettering. The railroad's name in stylized lettering was used in lieu of a herald. The Nickel Plate used the same approach and basic color scheme. *D&RGW: Don Sims; NKP: Koester*

exceptions to suggest that advice should not become engraved in stone.

The key learning point with the Rio Grande/Nickel Plate comparison is that very different railroads often share similar characteristics. Determining what they are and then using them to enhance the plausibility of a freelanced railroad is likely to be a good investment of time.

The Wheeling Way

In recent years, the remarkable sharing of attributes between the Rio Grande and Nickel Plate took a bizarre twist in the resurrection of the Wheeling & Lake Erie as a corporate entity.

The original Wheeling was a coal hauler that extended from Toledo southeast to the coalfields around Dillonvale, Ohio. It tapped the greater Pittsburgh area through a direct connection with the Pittsburgh & West Virginia, and it also had a line that ran south from the Lake Erie ports of Huron and Cleveland, Ohio, to Zanesville, thus forming the "Iron Cross."

The Nickel Plate leased the Wheeling in 1949 to form the Greater Nickel Plate system. It hauled coal west and iron ore east, and it was a key part of the Alphabet Route between the Midwest and East Coast. But after the

N&W merger, the old Wheeling main line fell out of favor.

A former Rio Grande executive, Larry R. Parsons, saw value in the Wheeling, acquired part of it, and resurrected its original name. After some less than graphically successful experiments, he adopted a painting and lettering scheme, **1**, that was a near clone of that of his former employer, which by this time had disappeared into an expanded Southern Pacific and then Union Pacific.

In the process, the WLE acquired some ex-Rio Grande tunnel motors, which were units with lowered air intakes to tap into the cooler air near the bottom of tunnels. No tunnel motors were bought new by the big Eastern coal haulers, but they're now increasingly common and hence a bit less intrusive on a freelanced Appalachian coal road, **7**.

Applying the Wheeling lessons

If there has ever been a sterling example of prototype-based freelancing, the modern Wheeling & Lake Erie is it! Resurrect an old railroad name, borrow another railroad's unused graphics, combine the two, and you're in business.

As we discussed in Chapter 6, this has important implications for the freelancer. He or she could buy a factory-painted unit, have custom road-name decals printed, and quickly create a roster of highly plausible-looking models with minimal effort and added expense.

In fact, I did exactly that when I created the Allegheny Midland. Like the Nickel Plate Road, its freight equipment and locomotives were lettered with the railroad's nickname: Midland Road. It was planned as an extension of the NKP's Wheeling District into West Virginia and a connection with Allen McClelland's Virginian & Ohio.

When I discovered that acquiring and upgrading the needed steam fleet would have been prohibitively expensive and difficult in the early 1980s, I dieselized the railroad. By building a railroad that was controlled

5

Rio Grande's *Yampa Valley Mail*, shown at top descending the Front Range on its trip back from Craig to Denver over the original Moffat Road line on August 13, 1966, is very similar to NKP trains 9 and 10 (bottom): a single Alco PA-1 powering a short train. Nickel Plate's overnight Cleveland–St. Louis trains 9 and 10 also served a line that branched off from the principal main line.
D&RGW: J.W. Swanburg; NKP: Joe Collias

Starting in 1950, the NKP received a number of Pullman-Standard lightweight passenger coaches, 10-6 sleepers, and two bedroom-buffet-lounges (including car 150, shown at top on the Wabash in Lafayette, Ind., in September 1965) that were very similar to cars built for the Chesapeake & Ohio. Over the years, some of the P-S cars served other railroads. The Rio Grande had several types of these cars, including the combine seen in the bottom photo on No. 9 at Rollins, Colo., on Oct. 8, 1967.
D&RGW: Bruce Black; Chuck Conway Collection

Using tunnel motors such as this SD40T-2 on an Appalachian railroad like the Allegheny Midland (left) was a bit of a stretch back in the 1980s. By the 2000s, ex-D&RGW and SP tunnel motors were increasingly common in the East, shown at right on the Algers, Winslow & Western in southern Indiana in September 2005, although not on the major railroads.

by the NKP, all units could be painted in the NKP livery but with "Midland" replacing "Nickel Plate." This meant I could slightly modify factory-painted locomotives and cars or use commercial NKP decal striping sets, **8**.

This was long before the "new Wheeling" emerged, but the same logic later applied by Larry Parsons—stick closely to an existing paint scheme—proved beneficial.

Filling out the roster
Choices, so many choices. Today, it's more a matter of what we really need to create a well-defined roster than what is available.

The concern for prototype modelers is whether a given model is sufficiently accurate and represents a locomotive or car that operated within their chosen era. Freelancers seemingly have much wider choices, but as layout-design guru John Armstrong once quipped, that simply makes it harder to make informed choices: The modeler needs to know not about only one railroad but about all of the similar railroads in the modeled region and time period.

Confining choices in this way makes prototype-based freelancing a more economical approach to scale modeling than a more liberal view of freelancing affords. By choosing the NKP as

the base prototype for the Midland Road, I could make more informed decisions about locomotive, caboose, and rolling stock types and ownerships than would have been the case had I simply decided that the AM was an Appalachian coal hauler.

It pays to have a Plan B railroad in your portfolio. The NKP was not involved in pulpwood traffic from loading yard to paper mill, for example, so I looked to the C&O for suitable pulpwood flat prototypes. Along with the Pere Marquette and Erie, the C&O and NKP had once been in the same Van Sweringen family of railroads, so that was not much of a stretch.

Like the Rio Grande tunnel motor hiding in plain sight between a pair of Wheeling & Lake Erie semi-clones (photo **1**), a Midland Road RSD-12 blends in with its Nickel Plate siblings (Overland RSD-12s) on the author's Allegheny Midland. Units factory-painted for the NKP such as this Atlas Alco were easy to re-letter for the Midland Road.

1

CHAPTER EIGHT

Planning and modeling structures

Randy Laframboise is accurately modeling the Rutland Railroad as it appeared in the early 1950s. This view of Brandon, Vt., shows a mix of scratchbuilt railroad structures and industrial buildings such as the coal dealer (inset photo, which I shot in September 2013) with repainted commercial houses. This ensures that recognizable key structures are in place, but time is not wasted on background buildings that play a supporting role. *Randy Laframboise*

Rewarding as adding highly detailed structures to a model railroad can be, **1**, there's no getting around the fact that they are merely part of the scenery, playing a supporting role to the main characters—the trains—in our miniature worlds. Ideally, we want to enjoy the construction of the scenery and structures that provide a context for the trains while also having an operational railroad. But we need to keep our eye on the ball and not spend so much time on the sideshow that we neglect the main event.

2 Despite my quest for authenticity, I have little idea how downtown Metcalf, Ill., looked during the 1950s. Most structures are no longer standing or are highly modernized. So, rather than leaving bare building lots in town, I am using relatively stock commercial kits to serve as stand-ins unless and until more information surfaces.

Size matters

If you're building a small railroad, you'll probably have time to do things that those of us building basement empires can only dream about. Scratchbuilding each and every structure, **1** and **6-11**, to precisely match its prototype is not something that I will have time to do in the foreseeable future—even if I had the needed information, which I don't.

On the other side of the ledger, on a large railroad every model is not scrutinized as carefully as on a small layout. The larger the layout, the less likely it becomes that a solitary model will be the star of the show.

If I were building, say, a one-town railroad fed by one or two staging/fiddle yards in Proto:48 (O fine-scale; see **2-12**), a primary objective would be to sweat the details. No sense going to the trouble to get the track gauge and wheel profile precisely correct if other parameters are compromised to any degree.

But I'm not doing that. What I am doing represents an entire subdivision. True, I have room to model only 8 scale miles of that 111-mile-long subdivision, but those portions of it that I elected to

model should evoke the actual locations sufficiently for a knowledgeable visitor (including me!) to be able to recognize them. That's the idea behind Layout Design Elements, which we briefly discussed in Chapter 1.

Moreover, I simply do not have much if any information on a lot of the structures that were located within modeling distance of the NKP main line. Always helpful Sanborn fire insurance plats, **4-5**, tell me that there was a two-story brick bank building in Metcalf, Ill. But it's not there now, and no photo I've found to date shows it. As such, it's a poor prospect for scratchbuilding.

What to do? I could plunk down any old brick store kit and call it a day. Better still would be to have it resemble a small-town bank, **2**. If a photo shows up, I'll reconsider.

In some cases, I do know what at least one or two sides of a building looked like. Take the Maple Hotel just west of the Nickel Plate depot in Charleston, Ill., for example. Thanks to a photo in the collection of my friend and NKP Clover Leaf District authority Steve Grigg, I know what

the east and south walls looked like. From a Sanborn map, I know the shape of its footprint. Assembling a generic hotel building kit is therefore not a good path forward, but neither is scratchbuilding it when 50 percent of the structure remains a mystery.

My first task was therefore to find a kit that had similar architectural attributes: brick, two stories, similar window treatments, and so forth. It pays to study the Walthers catalog like a college textbook in the hopes of later recalling a structure that will serve as a good starting point for such projects.

I suspected one of the Design Preservation Models kits, now produced by Woodland Scenics, was the answer. Bingo—a pair of Cutting's Scissors Co. kits looked like a good place to start.

The finished model, **3**, is certainly not an exact model of the prototype, but that isn't necessary for it to look the part. It's more than close enough to represent the Maple Hotel. And should additional information surface, I can always replace it with a more accurate model.

It pays not to pay too much heed

3

I kitbashed the Maple Hotel in Charleston, Ill. (top) using two Design Preservation Models (Woodland Scenics) Cutting's Scissor Co. kits (bottom) based on information in the prototype photo showing the east and south walls. Fortunately, the front and west walls are not readily visible on my HO railroad. *Prototype photo courtesy Steven Grigg*

4 The Swift soybean processing plant in Frankfort, Ind., now operated by ADM, was a relatively easy kitbashing project using Walthers cement plant silos and corrugated walls plus some styrene to represent concrete sections.

5 Jim Leighty photographed and then used both kitbashing and scratchbuilding techniques to build his semi-freelanced model of the huge Bradford lime plant at Bellefonte, Pa. It ships boxcars of bagged lime and covered hopper loads of bulk lime. Coal for heat-drying the lime provides some inbound loads. Measuring 8 feet long but only 2½" deep, it's a combination of buildings that once graced a friend's layout that were creatively modified and rearranged—a testimonial to the fun and potential of kitbashing!
Jim Leighty

to the label on the box. Hiding inside a Walthers kit that was labeled as a cement plant was actually the wherewithal for a soybean plant, **4**.

It also pays not to throw anything away. Jim Leighty salvaged several structures from a friend's layout just before they were tossed out and skillfully arranged them to resemble a lime plant he had photographed in Pennsylvania, **5**.

Structure data from maps
I mentioned the value of Sanborn fire insurance maps when it comes to obtaining footprint dimensions and

other information about structures. Valuation maps are almost as valuable in that regard.

When the Government assumed control of U.S. railroads during World War I, they sent out teams of surveyors to document everything they now "owned." The result of this humungous effort was a series of valuation maps showing every linear inch of the rail network, and that included the locations and footprints of lineside structures, **6**. When combined with information gleaned from Sanborn maps and photos, a blueprint for building reasonably accurate models can be created.

Scratchbuilding for the fun of it
There is a concern that modelers as a whole are losing the ability to build models from scratch. I don't think that's true. But the closing of brick-and-mortar hobby shops isn't helping, as this makes it more difficult to get the bits and pieces needed to scratchbuild a model.

Scratchbuilding remains of the most rewarding aspects of our hobby. Watching a miniature of an actual structure take shape before your eyes is an amazingly rewarding experience, **7**. Bonus: You won't even have to read the instructions!

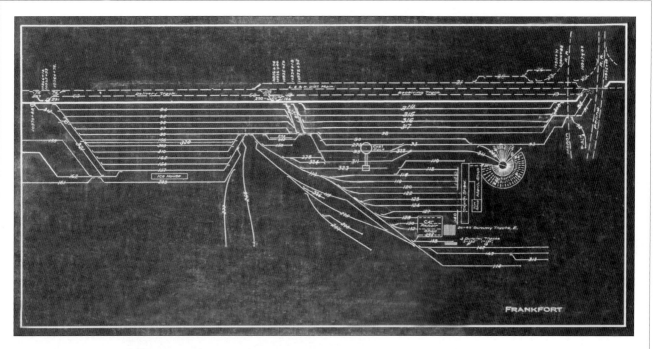

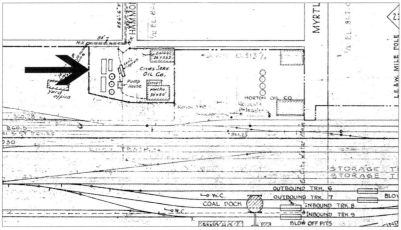

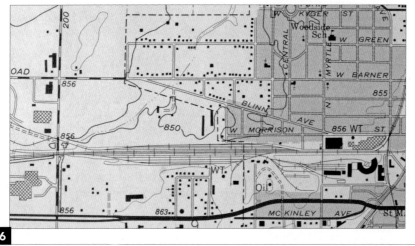

6

Taken together, information gleaned from railroad track diagram books, valuation maps, U.S. Geological Survey topographic maps, and photos form a good picture of how things looked—here at Frankfort, Ind., around 1950. The arrow points to the Cities Service fuel dealership, which is also visible in the photo. *Topographic map; U.S. Geological Survey; photo courtesy Jay Williams, Big Four Graphics*

But then so is kitbashing. It's a lot like assembling a puzzle: You start with odd pieces and wind up with something entirely new that closely resembles a desired model.

Structure mock-ups

Before diving too deeply into structure modeling, especially where large buildings are involved, we should consider building scale-size mock-ups of key structures. We may find that they don't fit without causing other concerns such as blocking one's ability to reach in to throw a switch or uncouple a car, **8**.

Jeff Kraker is modeling the Mann's Creek in West Virginia, which delivered coal and lumber to coke

The C&O's depot at Sproul, W.Va. (left), was a rewarding scratchbuilding project. No drawings existed, so I started with a cardstock mock-up to check measurements that I estimated from common window and door sizes and batten spacing (above).

7

8

Concerned about foreground structures blocking his ability to spot or uncouple cars, Mike Bowline constructed mock-ups of key structures. They also made early operations more realistic. *Mike Bowline*

9

Jeff Kraker, who models in On3, is another advocate of structure mock-ups, especially when they're foreground structures like a large company store that may become view blocks or impediments to operation. *Jeff Kraker*

ovens and an interchange with the Chesapeake & Ohio in Sewell. He built several structure mock-ups, **9**, to see how they will affect operations. Jeff offered several observations about this process:

"In the smaller scales," Jeff said, "structures usually don't have as big an impact on operations as in the larger scales. A depot between the aisle and the main line, for example, is seldom much cause for concern. But in O scale, a structure can be a significant view block and operating obstacle.

"Since my layout is set at a high elevation to go over a concrete wall, my two mining towns are at neck level. In one mining town, I had a two-story company store located between the aisle and the runaround tracks. I also had two company houses between the edge of the layout and the main line."

For the company houses, Jeff was able to find a small, one-story design. "I will slope the scenery down toward the fascia so the houses will be set halfway down, making them even lower. The two-story company store is a structure on my 'must build' list,

however. It's one of those structures that really defines the company-town image—the big store looming over all the small company houses showing 'who's boss.' But that building is a major view block and right in the middle of the runaround and in front of the tipple. So I needed to know if I could tolerate it before I built it.

"I built the mock-up and have it in place to see how it fits," he concluded. "If I decide that I just can't deal with that imposing structure, I will consider rerouting the tracks to move the store to the back."

1

CHAPTER NINE

Construction and maintenance

One of two main aisles on my HO tribute to the Nickel Plate Road's St. Louis Division in the fall of 1954 shows a series of magazine storage boxes at left under the Peoria Division staging yard. Like most other storage containers under the railroad, they are mounted on casters so they can be rolled out of the way when working under the railroad.

It may seem odd to cover construction and maintenance this late in the book, but these aspects come well after the planning is well along. We'll look at facets of a layout's physical form that can make it easier, or harder, to build and maintain. None of us is getting any younger, and what seemed like a good idea when we were in our 40s or 50s may turn into a major hassle as we pass the age-60 mark, **1**. A model railroad can last several decades, so we need to consider how well what we build will endure over time as well as how well we will endure over the same period.

2

The broad plain in front of the Frankfort operator's desk—actually the top of a knee wall that accommodates the hood of a car—would be difficult for the Frankfort Commercial Engine to switch. I used it to underscore the agricultural economy of the area served by the railroad.

Benchwork

Few of us rank benchwork at the top of our Fun Things To Do Today list, but it's actually very easy to build. As the late Jim Boyd often said, "You can fill an entire gymnasium with benchwork in a long weekend!"

For that matter, you can buy prefabricated benchwork from Sievers and other firms, or you can hire a custom layout builder to erect it—and keep going from there until you yell "Stop!" if you so desire. (See "Layout design help," on page 80, which also includes a sampling of sources of layout-design software programs.)

The learning point is that any kind of sturdy benchwork from conventional grid to L-girder will do the job. I prefer conventional grid built from 1 x 4s, but I have the 1 x 4s cut from ¾" plywood to ensure against warping and knots.

For upper decks, however, the thickness of the benchwork becomes a major liability. Every inch there subtracts from the clearance between decks. Conventional grid or L-girder benchwork is not a good choice.

Planning ahead

I confess that I don't always or even usually do things in a logical order. When I'm in the mood to do something—build benchwork, lay track, build structures, weather cars—I do it. My reasoning is that it's better to get something done than to continually drag my feet as I contemplate doing something that really needs to be done but looks like a tough job.

But long experience has taught me a thing or two about priorities as well as about things that look like fun but may not be practical. A case in point is the broad area between the main line and the Frankfort operator's desk on my HO railroad. This expanse spans the nose of my car, as it used to be the back of our garage.

At some point in time, a candy manufacturing plant was built on the west outskirts of Frankfort, Ind., and I seriously considered using this area to accommodate it. But as regular operating sessions commenced, I saw how much congestion there was in that aisle. Moreover, the busy operator would not appreciate someone hanging over his shoulder as he or she switched the candy plant. I decided it would be smarter to dedicate that area to scenery; a farm would be ideal, **2**.

Multi-deck railroads

Multi-deck layouts (also see Chapter 2) require more planning than single-deck railroads, if for no other reason than there's usually twice as much railroad to build, operate, and maintain. But an upper deck introduces certain construction procedures that may not initially be obvious.

What you need to know about multi-deck model railroads is covered in my book, *Designing and Building Multi-deck Model Railroads* (Kalmbach, 2008). But let me offer a few key points here as you contemplate whether more than one deck may help you achieve the objectives for your next model railroad.

Lighting the lower deck(s) should govern the design of the upper deck(s) infrastructure. When determining the spacing between decks, the thickness of the upper-deck benchwork or subroadbed becomes an issue. One has to allow not only for the thickness

of the subroadbed and supporting structure but also for the lighting system for the lower deck(s), **2-5**.

I used ¾" birch plywood for the subroadbed. Tempting as it may be to buy something that is on sale, save such foibles for things that are easily replaced when you can afford better material. This is especially important where basic infrastructure is concerned. I use ¾" cabinet-grade birch plywood for my subroadbed, for example. When asked why, I say that's because I couldn't find any 1"-thick plywood.

Subroadbed thickness is a function of riser spacing. I space my risers 16" apart, the same distance specified for studs in house walls. I know from hard-won experience that spacing risers 24" apart under ¾" plywood will allow the plywood to sag over time.

Yes, you may get away with using thinner plywood, or a cheaper grade of plywood, or locating risers farther apart. Then again, you may not. Why take a chance to save a few bucks?

Those of you who use spline roadbed will probably be able to span greater distances between supports, as the vertical dimension of such roadbed is usually an inch or greater. If you use 2" insulating foam panels for your subroadbed, Maumee Route builder Bill Darnaby agrees with my recommendation for plywood that supports be spaced no farther than 16" apart. But remember that the added thickness of spline or foam roadbed will subtract from the spacing between decks.

In most areas, I supported the plywood with inexpensive, stamped-metal shelf brackets, visible in photo **2-5**. This allowed me to easily attach the under-cabinet fluorescent fixtures used to evenly illuminate the lower deck. The fluorescent fixtures I used range from around ¾" to 1½" in thickness; the thinner ones are under the ¾" x 18"-long splice plates between the 8-foot lengths of subroadbed.

I use mostly cool-white fluorescent lamps (tubes), which range in temperature from 4100 to 4300 Kelvin. I installed a few "colder" (less red) 5000K lamps as experiment, but I noted no improvement in colors, and

they're more expensive and harder to get on a weekend, which is when you'll usually discover several tubes are flickering or burned out. Lighting experts are concerned with a tube's CRI, or color rendition index; I have never noticed any problems with color shift while using cool-white lamps.

By the way, the photos of my NKP layout in this book were all taken with normal layout lighting using a digital camera set to Auto White Balance.

Fluorescents do emit ultraviolet (UV) rays, which can cause colors to fade over time. That used to be a concern with some brands of ground foam, which turned brown and disintegrated, but this doesn't seem to be a problem today. Libraries and museums slide the fluorescent lamps into plastic sleeves that absorb the UV, but in my long experience this is overkill for a model railroad. If you print out your own photo backdrops, however, it's important to use UV-resistant inks.

Continuing advances in light-emitting diodes suggest thin strips of LEDs will become the norm. Just be aware that unless the LEDs shine through a diffuser, you may see narrow bands or stripes of light shining on the railheads. That can be distracting.

Vertically deep scenes

If you're new to multi-deck layout planning, beware of vertically deep scenes on the upper deck(s). As is evident in the accompanying photos, **3**, a "signature" bridge scene on my railroad projected down toward the lower deck. I had just enough room to have the lower-deck main line "tunnel" under the base of the river and bridge on the middle deck.

Wiring wisdom

Plan ahead! That's crucial advice when it comes to wiring the upper deck. I didn't want to have the two track bus wires dangling from the lower surface of the upper deck, so I ran feeders (one for every rail!) down behind the backdrop to bus wires located below the lower deck, **2-5**. That's a lot easier to do before the lower-deck's backdrop is installed.

The middle-deck Little Vermilion River bridge scene near Humrick, Ill., was a tight fit. Using two panels (of three) of Micro Engineering's bridge tower kits allowed just enough clearance for the Toledo and Sandusky divisions' main lines to pass below. A black-and-white photocopy of the color backdrop, printed from a scan of a color slide I shot in 1967, was used to plan how to crop the $55 color print.

3

It's a good idea to color code the bus wires (with tags) and the power districts (with felt-tip markers) on a plan of your railroad. You can then tell at a glance which sections of the railroad are powered by which booster.

Bear in mind that you may want to have each deck in different power districts so that a short circuit on the one deck doesn't affect trains on the other. And make sure you understand the wiring requirements for any signalizing systems you may plan to install at a later date. "Fishing" wires down behind an installed backdrop can be a major pain, as I have repeatedly rediscovered.

A power district is that part of your railroad that is powered by one DCC command station or booster. It's a good idea to use electronic circuit breakers (ECBs) to further divide the layout into smaller powered sections to limit the effect of a short.

If you use conventional DC wiring, each block is in effect its own electrical district.

Dividing the railroad into power districts or blocks makes it much easier to troubleshoot a problem. This also helps to ensure that an ECB can successfully reset after a short has

been cleared, even if there are several locomotives equipped with power-hungry sound decoders in that district.

Add labels to your bus wires—Power District Blue, for example—that match a color-coded track plan showing the limits of each power district, **4**.

Speaking of color coding, you may be as surprised as I was to learn that while less than 1 percent of females have some degree of color blindness, something like 14 percent of males are so afflicted. One of the towns on my layout had "target" (one light that changes colors) train-order signals, which are indecipherable to a few of my regular crew. The solution was to build a panel with levers that show how the signals are set.

Semaphore signals are obviously easy for someone who is color blind to read. But signal heads with one lens for each color can be read as long as crews know that the top light is red or green, which varies by railroad.

Track tips

I enjoy handlaying track, and on the Allegheny Midland all but hidden staging yard track was handlaid code 70 and 83 track. For the Nickel Plate, I used Micro Engineering codes 55 and 70 flextrack.

Rail thicker than code 83, such as code 100, is actually too tall for prototypical HO use on all but the heaviest-duty main lines. The most common rationale for buying "oversize" code 100 flextrack is that it is cheaper than more realistic rail sizes such as codes 70 and 83. But it remains popular because of its availability, cost, strength, and durability.

When painted and weathered, code 100 rail doesn't look bad, but as you gain more experience and knowledge of prototype practices, the relatively huge rail may bother you. Replacing it after the track has been ballasted and scenery is in place would be a major task.

I chose to use flextrack because of the detail molded into each tie:

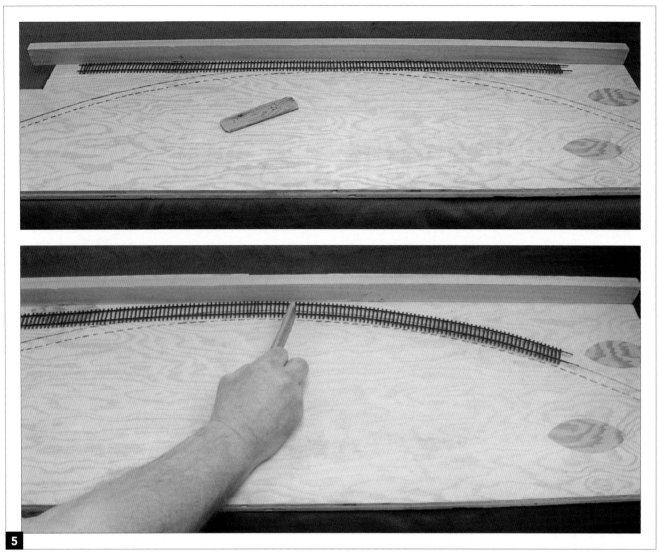

5

Curving Micro Engineering's weathered-rail flextrack is easy if you place the track against a backstop and gently batter the ends of the ties toward the center. It will gradually assume the desired radius and can be adjusted into a perfect arc by eye.

wood grain, tie plates, and spikes. You can achieve comparable detail with handlaid track (check the products sold by the Proto:87 Stores, for example), but I was not willing to spend that much time when laying well over a thousand feet of track.

In the August 2003 *Model Railroader*, Chuck Hitchcock described how he used DAP clear adhesive caulk to glue flextrack to the roadbed. I tried some other brands and discovered that I should have paid closer attention to his recommendations. DAP adhesive caulk seems to achieve a "tack" that holds the track in place immediately, especially on curves.

I prefer to use Micro Engineering's weathered flextrack. True, it is harder to curve, but that turns out to be an advantage. As shown in photo **5**, I place the track against a backstop attached to a sheet of plywood and use a piece of wood to rub inward from either end against the tie ends. This gently batters them toward the center of the desired arc, and the weathered rail helps to retain this curve. Minor adjustments by eye to ensure a smooth curve are still required.

Turnouts and crossings

I handlaid all turnouts on the AM, but for the Nickel Plate layout I used several different types of turnouts. The yard at Frankfort, Ind., comprises mostly Micro Engineering no. 6 turnouts. The turnouts at the east end of Cayuga, Ind., are handlaid. All mainline turnouts are no. 8, and most of them are modified Shinohara code 70 no. 8s, **6**.

I belatedly discovered the utility of the turnout tie strips sold by Central Valley. They can be curved by snipping off the webs between the ties along one side of the tie strip, **7**, although I was careful not to do that around the frog, as that section must remain straight. Using these versatile tie strips allowed me to build a curved yard ladder at Charleston, Ill., which in turn allowed me to use no. 8 turnouts where I had planned to use only no. 6s.

Central Valley also makes tie strips for mainline track and sidings. I use a 12" length of their newer mainline tie strips out of each of the three routes from their turnout tie strips, as the raised pins help align the rail before

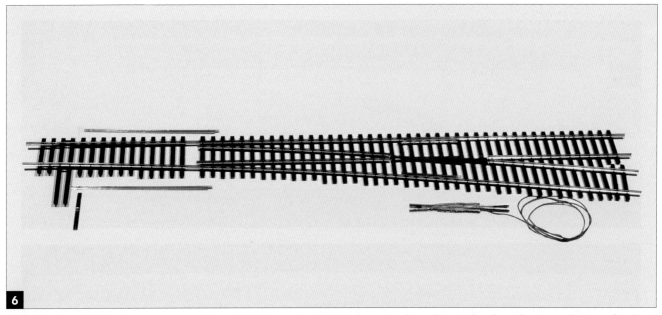

6

Modifying an old Shinohara turnout to allow the points to be spaced more closely to the stock rails without any danger of a short circuit caused by a passing metal wheel is not difficult: Replace the metal "throw bars" with a Clover House PC strip, remove and clean up the points and solder them to the closure rails, and gap the frog. Here the frog is being replaced with a Details West manganese-insert type frog, which is typical of most mainline frog castings.

7

Central Valley turnout tie strips can be curved by removing the inner web between the ties, but leave the ties near the frog straight. Details West frogs are designed to fit on these tie strips, but the flangeways may need to be slightly deepened. Curved no. 8 turnouts thus fit nicely in a ladder on my railroad in an area designed for straight no. 6 turnouts.

it is spiked down. The pins are to be peened over to form rail anchors and secure the rail to the tie strips, but I also drive small spikes alongside each rail anchor for added security. The plastic ties are hollow, making it relatively easy to push in the small spikes.

As luck would have it, there is not a single 90-, 45-, or 30-degree crossing in any of the towns I chose to model. Rather than compromise the geometry of each crossing, I am building custom diamonds based on crossing angles I obtained from railroad drawings or estimated from U.S. Geological Society quadrangle maps.

Building a working crossing diamond is not easy task, and I wasn't about to get bogged down building a dozen or so such crossings as I pushed toward the inaugural operating session. I therefore butted the rails of the dummy crossing railroad's track to either side of the NKP main line, **8**. I will go back and install the missing running and guard rails as time permits.

I cut rail gaps with a thin cutoff disk in a hand motor tool (while wearing protective goggles, of course!), then dip thin strips of dark gray Plastruct ABS into thick cyanoacrylate adhesive (CA) and slide them into the gaps, **9**. I trim them off and file them to shape after the CA dries.

Duckunders

Duckunders that were a mere annoyance yesterday may become a physical impediment tomorrow. I installed short railings on either side of the 48"-high duckunder that the Charleston yardmaster and roundhouse foreman/hostler need to negotiate at least twice during each operating session, **10**. Putting your weight on the railings via your arms rather than on your back is much more comfortable.

To save time as I pushed toward regular operating sessions, I simply butted unpowered foreign-road tracks against the NKP main line. I'll later finish the dummy crossings, perhaps using cast-resin rail.

To insulate gaps in the rail, dip thin Plastruct gray ABS strips in thick CA, push them into gaps cut with a thin cut-off disk in a motor tool, and later trim them with flush rail cutters, a hobby knife, and a file.

I added wood railings along both sides of a 48"-high duckunder to relieve stress on the back (left). Neil Schorr has built a beautiful 3-rail layout to O scale standards. To avoid a duckunder when entering the railroad room, Neil had a depressed stair well constructed complete with authentic Pennsylvania railings (above). *Neal Schorr*

An increasing number of modelers now use photo backdrops. They nicely extend the horizon on this 16"-wide scene. The legal-size sheets are from SceniKing, and they now offer 6-foot-long Roll Out panels.

Painting both sides of Masonite tempered hardboard with latex paint does not seal it from moisture and hence expansion and contraction. In the dry winter months, my backdrop develops small cracks, even when using flexible spackle. I should have sealed the hardboard with polyurethane or a marine varnish.

Modelers have employed everything from swinging gates or lift-out sections to depressed floors (also see photo **10**) to avoid having to bend over. Duckunders can be avoided entirely if access to the layout room is via stairs that come into the center of the floor.

Backdrop construction

Backdrops have become increasingly important now that modelers are using photo backdrops (see "Photo backdrops" at right) to extend the apparent distance between the railroad and the distant horizon, **11**. But this has raised some construction concerns.

The backdrop material must be stiff enough to resist buckling as panels of photos are bonded to the backdrop. Whereas relatively thin styrene or linoleum makes an excellent backdrop for those who intend to paint it blue and add simple details, those materials may prove problematic when you attempt to glue digital photos to them. As always, build a test section before you commit to a specific material and methodology.

I learned the hard way that I should have (1) sealed my hardboard

backdrop panels on both sides with a polyurethane coating (not porous latex paint, **12**) and (2) installed the backdrops as soon as I finished installing the benchwork. Instead, I installed the subroadbed, roadbed, and track, then tried to maneuver the ⅛"-thick sheets of hardboard into place. Since the backdrop sections for the lower deck had to be notched to fit around the L-shaped brackets that supported the upper deck, it was not a simple matter to slide them into place. Several sections of flextrack had to be pried loose and thrown away due to damage caused when installing the backdrop panels.

Tick, tick, tick...

Nothing is as easy as it looks, but then nothing is usually as hard as we fear. And one thing is certain: We won't get anything done if we don't give it a shot.

For example, you may be stymied by indecision as to which is the "best" DCC system to buy. It's like buying a desktop or laptop computer; it all depends. My advice is to go with whatever the other modelers in your area are using, as they will have a lot of

hard-won knowledge and spare parts. You can pool throttles during operating sessions.

If no one in your neck of the woods has progressed to DCC, do an online search for chat groups devoted to each major brand and ask pointed questions. You'll get a mix of fact and opinion, but you'll quickly determine whether a given system has features that are critical to meet your needs or come up short. For example, if you will be consisting diesels during an operating session, you may find a system that makes that easier than others.

Photo backdrops

Here are several sources for photographic backdrops or software that allow you to print your own:
- Backdrop Junction: backdropjunction.com
- Backdrop Warehouse: backdropwarehouse.com
- Larc Products: larcproducts.com
- SceniKing: sceniking.com

CHAPTER TEN

Animation

The water plug that replenishes Yosemite Valley steam locomotives on Jack Burgess's HO railroad swings out over the track. It's powered by a 4-rpm Hankscraft (or Switchmaster) motor connected to the water plug by a length of brass tubing. A long steel pin through the tubing and motor shaft contacts nails positioned 90-degrees apart; the motor stalls in the stored or in-use position.
Jack Burgess

When someone mentions "animation" and "model railroad" in the same breath, a lot of us conjure up images of milk cans being unceremoniously tossed out of a Lionel reefer or cattle vibrating down a ramp from a stock car. Or maybe we see a detailed model of the week when the county fair came to town complete with Ferris wheels and Tilt-A-Whirls madly rotating amidst a blaze of colorful lights. But animation can be much more subtle than that, **1**, and still enhance a railroad that strives to depict the ordinary, mundane, everyday events that are typical of railroading in a given time and place.

What is "animation"?

To be sure we're all on the same page, let me offer a definition of animation: It encompasses everything that moves, or seems to move, including fluctuating light and sound waves. Something as simple as a switch stand target that rotates 90 degrees as the switch points are moved is an excellent example of the value of animation.

The "need" for animation is most likely a function of its overall impact on the appearance and performance of a model railroad. Compare a smaller railroad, where the builder is more likely to have the time to employ various forms of animation and the viewer is more likely to notice them, to a large railroad where there is so much to take in that the smaller details may be overlooked.

Signaling

Signals are a highly useful and attention-getting form of animation, **2**. The old semaphore signals are especially eye-catching. Circuitron of Tortoise switch motor fame now sells the Smail, which is designed for use with Digital Command Control and can position a semaphore blade of a block or train-order signal at the red, yellow, or green positions. It will also raise and lower crossing gates. And firms like Tam Valley offer servos that take little room and offer the precise alignment adjustments needed to accurately, and repeatedly, position a signal arm.

Iowa Scaled Engineering makes Interlocking in a Box (IIAB), a development I've been anticipating for years, which can handle the signaling requirements of a crossing at grade. Both crossings can be active or one line can be a short dummy main line. In the latter case, **3**, the schedules of foreign-road trains supposedly crossing the modeled railroad's main line can be programmed in. So if a "dummy" railroad's train is supposed to cross your railroad's main at, say, 10 a.m., the IIAB circuitry will check to see whether one of your trains is within interlocking limits (between the distant and home signal) and, if not, knock down your railroad's home signals to

2 Operating signals and lights on locomotives (note the cab interior lighting) can add considerable interest and drama, as is evident in this photo of David Stewart's original O scale Appalachian & Ohio. Photographer Bob Sobol reports that there are 14 LEDs on this F3 to illuminate the instrument panel, cab reading lights, ground lights, number boards, class lights, and four sealed-beam headlights. *Bob Sobol*

3 Interlocking in a Box, from Iowa Scaled Engineering, controls the home signals at an interlocked crossing when both routes over the diamond are active or when one is a dummy route. The schedules of "ghost" foreign-road trains—here the Monon crossing my NKP at Linden, Ind.—can be programmed into the system. It can also trigger a recording (from another vendor) of a train hammering over the diamond(s).

red-over-red for a set period.

On my Nickel Plate, there are eight locations where a foreign-road train could cross over the NKP main. NKP engineers therefore have to be vigilant as they approach an interlocking plant

to be sure the route is clear. That adds to the action on a typical run over the subdivision.

A future add-on to the Interlocking in a Box could be having the IIAB play a recording of a long or short train

Paul Dolkos photographed this manually operated gate or smash board guarding the CSX-NS diamond at Dock Junction in Brunswick, Ga., in February 2010 (left). A model gate could be rotated manually or by a motor. A rotating smash board with lighted signal atop protects the crossing of the Boston Track with the enginehouse lead on Perry Squier's 1923 HO edition of the Pittsburg, Shawmut & Northern. Here it's lined for the lead.

Bill Darnaby controls most of the interlocking systems on his Maumee Route using Hump Yard Purveyance levers. Moving a lever actuates a switch that triggers a Digitrax SE8c signal driver. *Bill Darnaby*

Jack Burgess rigged the rods from the tower to the semaphore home signals and split-point derails to move when an approaching train covers a sensor, automatically clearing the route for a YV train. This favors the (theoretically) much busier Santa Fe route through the interlocking plant. *Jack Burgess*

behind a steam or diesel locomotive passing over the crossing during the period that the modeled railroad's home signal is set at stop (and stay stopped).

Interlocking crossings were once commonly protected by "smash boards," which swung out to block one of the routes through a crossing. Similarly, the Pittsburg, Shawmut & Northern protected the crossing of a busy yard track with the engine leads by a rotating smash board, which Perry Squier has modeled and motorized on his HO railroad, **4**.

Bill Darnaby used logic software and Hump Yard Purveyance plastic interlocking "armstrong" levers to build interlocking plants for each of the many crossings on his HO railroad, **5**. He described the process in "Signaling with software" in *Model Railroad Planning 2010*.

Jack Burgess added working split-rail derails and operating semaphore home signals to his HO Yosemite Valley Railroad, **6**. Visit his website, yosemitevalleyrr.com, for more information on this remarkable railroad.

Automated interchanges

Iowa Scaled Engineering also makes an Automated Interchange (AI). I have two of them installed on the NKP, **7**. Power to a 30-car-long to-NKP interchange track is controlled by

7

Two interchanges on the author's railroad are controlled by Iowa Scaled Engineering Automated Interchange circuit boards. An infrared sensor between the ties detects the absence of cars after the Nickel Plate makes a pickup, restoring power (after a 23-minute delay) to locomotives on the delivering railroad's interchange track, which then shove another cut of cars into view. The first car again covers the IR sensor, cutting off power.

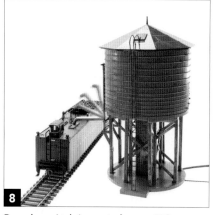

8

Broadway Ltd. Imports has an HO water tower with a spout that pivots down to the tender deck while appropriate tender hatch opening, closing, and rushing water sounds are heard.
Courtesy Broadway Ltd.

the AI circuitry; if the lead car of the to-NKP cut of cars covers an infrared sensor, power to the interchange track is off.

The 30-car cut of to-NKP cars is subdivided into 6- to 8-car blocks by pins in the knuckles of the last car in each block. When the NKP picks up the lead block of cars, that uncovers the IR sensor. After a time delay expires—I set mine at the maximum, 23 minutes—the interchange track is powered, and the foreign-road loco shoves another block of cars into view.

Sound

The most obvious advance in model railroading in recent times is Digital Command Control, or DCC, and with it realistic sound effects. The latter have progressed from locomotive-generated sounds—exhaust, bell, whistle or horn, etc.—to include decoders on freight cars that can simulate flange squeal, coupler clank, and so on.

From an operational standpoint, the ability to use the whistle or horn as a means of signaling is perhaps the most important feature. For example, if you're running a section (except the last one) of a train, you need to alert trains you pass or meet by blowing a long and two shorts and receiving an acknowledgement from the affected crew. If you're stopped at a manned interlocked crossing and grow impatient for the home signal to clear,

you can blow four shorts to alert the towerman that you're still waiting.

Sound also fosters more realistic train movements. I timed the interval between a train starting out in a yard until the caboose had cleared the last turnout with the sound turned off and then again with it turned on, and the difference was remarkable: The sound of the steam or diesel locomotive's exhaust caused the engineer to ease out much more slowly on the throttle, either because he was enjoying the sound or he didn't want to be caught racing out of town.

Miniaturization, small electric motors, tiny computer chips, and cell-phone speakers are allowing manufacturers and modelers to become ever more inventive with sound effects. I recently heard an N scale EMD Geep equipped with a Tsunami sound decoder feeding a thumbnail-size cell-phone speaker, and the volume and quality of the sound was virtually the same as on my HO Geeps.

SoundTraxx has already pioneered in under-layout sound, and this will only improve as ways to have the sounds follow train movements become more feasible. We can't readily tell from which direction low-frequency sounds are emanating, so a few big speakers around the layout room should suffice. These are the very sounds that small speakers do not produce, so it's win-win.

9

How long does it take to refill a tender with coal and water? Just push the buttons on the fascia and wait till the sound—generated by Miller Models (now ITT Products) circuit boards—stops.

Handheld throttle functionality

No longer does the engine hostler ask me how long it takes to fill a tender with coal or water. He simply positions the locomotive by the coal dock or water column and pushes the appropriate button, **8**. A digital sound module from Miller Models plays the appropriate sounds.

George Solovay (ittproducts.com), who manufactured the former Miller

A scratchbuilt Whiting Rotaside dumper that loads barges complements the King Coal preparation plant on David Stewart's Appalachian & Ohio. Twenty-car loaded O scale coal drags weigh in at 40 pounds, so the idea of fighting friction and gravity is not just colorful prose, and the pushers are not window dressing! *Two photos: Bob Sobol*

A model railroad loosely based on West Virginia's Mann's Creek narrow-gauge line in On3 resulted in wood hopper cars large enough for Jeff Kraker to equip each scratchbuilt hopper with tiny motors that open the side doors, thus allowing "coal" to dump into a bin below the tracks. *Jeff Kraker*

Models line, can supply any of those products on request at no additional charge. His HQ series of sound-effects modules has more than 150 sounds to choose from; for example, LT200 combines realistic lightning flashes with thunder sounds. George can also create customized sound modules.

The sound decoders in most steam locomotives also offer a water-loading sequence. But I don't want engineers pushing any buttons on handheld throttles that are not analogous to the functions an engineer would perform in a locomotive cab. So it's okay for him or her to open the throttle, turn lights on or off, set the brakes, blow the whistle or horn, and ring the bell. But in my view it's not appropriate for the engineer to use the throttle to initiate water-loading sounds or throw a switch remotely. Besides, he might push the wrong button and cause the engineer to be ejected through the cab roof hatch and float back to Earth under a tiny parachute.

Loading fuel and water

Just as we now have water towers with spouts that move up and down, **9**, and water columns that swing out over the tender-filling hatch, **1**, which would also work for fuel cranes, we may one day have coal docks that load our tenders with "coal."

A few modelers have already done this with coal tipples that load coal into hoppers and rotary dumpers that unload it into barges or ships, **10**.

I used "live" coal loads in hoppers on the Allegheny Midland, mainly to increase car weight to the point that pusher engines were required to get the trains up the mountain. Occasionally, a car would derail and dump the plastic coal all over the ground, but the main problems were (1) the load shape settled down as the cars moved, losing its realistic hump, and (2) coal granules occasionally fouled switch points and guard rails.

Jeff Kraker, who models the Mann's Creek in On3 (O scale, 3-foot-gauge), actually empties entire trains of wooden hopper cars by having an actuator turn on tiny motors in each car that open side doors, **11**, as a Shay

A small cityscape built by Erik Block and Evans Daes (see *Model Railroad Planning 2015*) includes automated vehicles that follow predetermined paths and operate brake lights and turn signals as required. The animation adds lots of action to a small HO exhibition layout. *Erik Block*

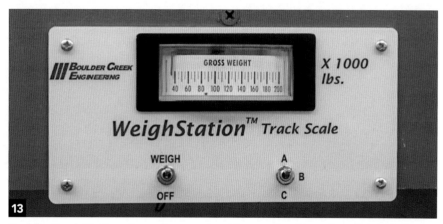

Boulder Creek Engineering makes a scale with an analog (shown) or digital read-out that detects the presence of a car on the scale track. Depending on how the toggle switch is set, it then shows a randomly selected loaded or empty weight for each car within preset, adjustable limits.

A flickering red fusee between the rails, made by LogicRail Technologies and activated by a pushbutton on the fascia, "burns" for an adjustable time (10 actual minutes on my railroad) to warn approaching trains that another train is stopped or working directly ahead.

15

A string of blue rope lights, as here on my railroad during a test to see how bright it is, or blue LEDs can create a pleasing moonlit night effect that makes building and vehicle lights and signals "pop." The rope lights were bright enough to operate trains but not to read paperwork.

moves the cars through the unloader.

Other opportunities exist to load and unload containers from flat and well cars, and scrap steel from gondolas using a crane equipped with an electromagnet.

I've seen working wreck cranes that swung from side to side, raised and lowered the boom, and moved the cables that raised and lowered the "big hook." It's not a stretch to think in terms of powering log-loading cranes and steam shovels that load coal into tenders.

Vehicles that move

Faller and others have produced vehicles that steer themselves around the "track," often in a surprisingly realistic manner. Erik Block and Evans Daes have employed their homegrown versions of such vehicles, complete with brake lights and turn signals, **12**, on at

least one of the small exhibition layouts they take to various European model railroad exhibitions.

"We used DC Car from Holland and Germany (www.miniatuura.nl), Erik reports. "They sell all kinds of products from the magnet strip and wooden profiles for the roads with a space to put the magnet strip into to all kind of wheels, batteries, and lamps. With their products, you can animate almost any vehicle.

"The only problem," he cautioned, "is getting the batteries inside. The smaller the vehicles the smaller the battery and the shorter it will last. In trucks, we use bigger ones that will last several hours.

"We also had to change the wheels on every vehicle," Erik concluded. "The front wheels had to be connected with a tie rod to turn, and all had to have rubber tires."

Track scales

"Loaded" boxcars or covered hoppers need to be weighed as they're shoved into the unloading area of a soybean plant, among other industries, and then again after they're emptied to determine the weight of product delivered. My bean plant crew doesn't actually weigh the cars, but they do spot them one at a time on a scale (well, over a to-be-built scale), where they are detected by an optical sensor. Depending on how a toggle switch is set on the Boulder Creek Engineering panel, **13**, the scale reads out a randomly chosen loaded or empty "weight" within a preset range.

Lighting effects

There is almost no limit to what can be accomplished with lighting effects, especially in conjunction with sounds. David Stewart arranged an alcove

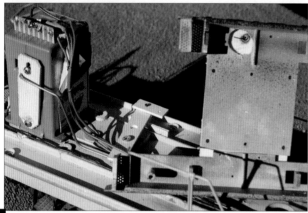

Bob Springs installed a Circuitron Tortoise switch motor and linkage in the ample confines of a 1:29 Geep's cab to have the engineer (not just his head) smoothly swing around to face forward or backward as the locomotive's direction is changed. *Bob Springs*

16

of his original Appalachian & Ohio to evoke images of a thunderstorm, complete with lightning and booming sound effects.

I recently installed the first of what will probably be a series of LogicRail (logicrail@att.net) "fusees" at key spots along the main line. The first two can protect either end of the busy switching locale of Cayuga, Ind. Crews working there can push a button on the fascia to trigger an adjustable-burn-time fusee, **14**, to protect them as they work. Mine are set at 10 actual minutes, the burning time of a typical fusee, as switching moves don't really scale down well in terms of elapsed time.

Equipping buildings with lights and dimming the main lighting to create a nighttime effect can be highly effective, even dramatic as daylight gradually fades and the blue hues of the night assume command. But this takes a lot of extra planning and installation work. It will impress the casual visitor but may irritate your operating crew.

One of the most effective examples of night lighting was created by the late Dan Zugelter on his beautiful HO rendition of the Chesapeake & Ohio in the Appalachians. Dan left a channel a few inches wide and deep between the tree-covered ridgeline and sky backdrop. In this slot were Christmas tree bulbs ranging from white to blue. A timer gradually reduced the white as the yellow, orange, red, and finally blue bulbs were turned on, then reversed that sequence. Spectacular! Dan's layout is currently stored in Hinton, W.Va., and is planned as a future display.

As an experiment, I strung a single string of blue rope lights alongside the fluorescent "day" lighting. When I turned off all room lights, the blue rope lights provided more than enough illumination to see what I was doing as I made some test runs, **15**. Blue LEDs should work equally well.

Moving figures

It's a bit disconcerting to see people or animals posed in positions that suggest

movement. That looks okay in still photos, but it looks ridiculous in videos and grows tiresome when we actually view a model railroad.

Track-planning guru John Armstrong had an engineer in an O scale locomotive that faced forward and then to the rear as the locomotive was reversed (November 1989 MR). Bob Springs accomplished much the same thing but a bit more smoothly in 1:29, **16**.

Viessmann (one website that shows their products is www.eurorailhobbies.com/viessmann.asp) now has a number of animated figures that can offer a partial cure for such ailments. Among them are chickens pecking at seed on the ground, a woman pumping water from a well, and a man sawing through a log.

The need for a below-layout mechanism precludes such innovations as a flagman swinging a red lantern or an engineer waving from the cab. But never underestimate the power of an innovative mind!

Learn More Essentials from a Model Railroad Expert

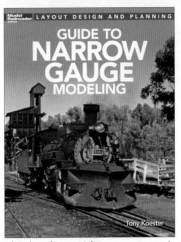
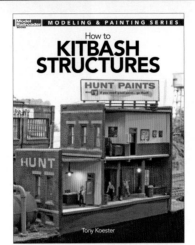
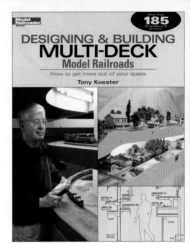
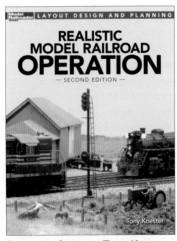

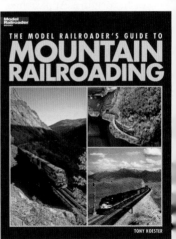